序　言

　　近年來國人出國旅遊的人數大增，因此在國外使用電話的機會也越來越多。雖然有不少人會説一般的英語會話，但是碰到要用到電話跟外國人交談時，不是冒出 "*I am Mr. David Lin. Glad to meet you.*" 讓對方啼笑皆非，就是緊張得張口結舌，滿頭大汗。這主要是因爲不熟悉電話英語特殊的語法，和慣用的句型、術語，當然説不出正確的句子來，(「我是林大衛」要説 "*This is Mr. David Lin speaking.*" 而且電話中不是見面，不能説 meet 。) 再加上雙方又不是面對面，無法了解對方表情反應，也不能用手勢輔助，才會有説錯或説不出來的情形。「電話英語」針對這幾項困難，提供國人一套迅速有效的學習方式。

　　本書以實況會話爲主體，分爲國內電話和國際電話兩大部分；取材涵蓋所有的場合與狀況。並配合必備的基本常識，讀過一遍就會應用。是出國觀光、業務考察、接待外賓不可或缺的得力助手。

　　一本書爲求完美，必須經過審慎的編輯，多次的校對，本書當然也不例外。但恐仍有疏漏，尚請各界先進不吝指教。

編者　謹識

Contents
目 錄

第 **1** 章 電話英語必備常識

" What You Need
to Know for
Telephone English "

聽比說更重要

人與人之間的談話，因場合不同，有時是一半一半的相互談話，有時則必須扮演完全的講者或聽衆。除了個人獨白的情形，其他情況都必須仔細聽對方的談話內容。有些人一邊聽對方談話。一邊就自顧自地考慮自己應該說些什麼，這實在是一種不禮貌的行爲。

所以，要達到一次成功、愉快的談話，*A good conversationist is a good listener.* 實在是至理名言，這不僅限於面對面的談話，就是在有限時間內溝通意見的電話交談中，也絕不容忽視。

當你聽不清楚對方說些什麼的時候，你可以說 *Beg your pardon*？但因在用電話交談的時候，往往因爲看不到對方，無法判斷對方的臉色而臨機應變，對方心情好，那一切都好辦，萬一對方心情不太好，你連續問幾次 *Beg your pardon*？可能引起對方不悅。但是這是訓練聽力上，不可避免的過程，只有義無反顧地秉持求眞的精神，建立聽的能力，才是上策。絕不能在未聽清楚其談話內容之前，就胡吹亂蓋起來。只要減慢自己的談話速度，對方會了解你的困難，儘量減慢速度或改用簡單的會話的。

「喂」的說法

Hello（喂）是電話交談的第一句話，要注意的是其重音在第二音節，發音是〔hɛ′lo〕。但有許多人發成〔′halo〕（ hollow 洞穴），或〔′hælo〕（ hallow 使神聖），就會遭人笑柄。雖然是要叫喚別人，引起別人的注意， Hello 常發成〔′hɛlo〕或改成 Hullo〔′hʌ′lo〕，但電話交談的 Hello，一定要將重音放在後面。

所謂「好的開始是成功的一半」（ *Well begun, half done.* ）一句好的開頭用語「 Hello 」可以使你的談話漸入佳境。

「我就是。」的說法

當對方要找的人就是自己的時候，我們說「我就是」，英文的說法是 *This is he.* 或 *This is she.* 千萬別直譯成 I am he（she）。由於對方問的是 *May I speak to Mr.（Miss.）~?* 所以也可以回答 *This is ~ speaking.* 也有人只說 *Speaking.*，尤其是工作繁忙的人。

當然簡略地說 *It's me.* 也無不可，但這種說法僅限用於熟識的朋友之間，如果對沒有交情的人用，可能給予對方突兀的感覺，在正式談話或談生意時最好不要使用。當然，若用 *Is it you ~?* 是想確定接電話的人就是自己要找的人。但不適用於談公事。

「您是哪一位？」不是 Who are you？

有許多問話是不能照中文直譯的，譬如「您有何貴幹？」可直接譯成 What is your business？也無不可，但這就帶有「你到底要幹什麼？」的語氣，顯得不夠禮貌。

同樣地，在電話交談中問「您是哪一位？」時，若用 Who are you？就相當於「喂，你是誰啊？」，不太合理，照中文的說法除了「您是哪一位」，也可以用「哪位…」或「對不起，您是…」，其英文的說法就是：

Who is calling, please？
Who is speaking, please？
Whom am I speaking to？
May I have your name？ 等等。

此外，若是董事長秘書接的電話，而對方想和董事長說話時，祕書必須問，「您是哪一位？」其英文是：*What name shall I give？*（*Who shall I say is calling, please？*）

可以在自己的名字之前加 Mr.

　　中文在說自己的名字時，絕不可以加上「先生」「小姐」「太太」等，但英文的某些場合，用 *Dr., Mr., Mrs., Miss* 之類的頭銜並不足爲奇，尤其是電話留言時，爲避免混淆，一定要請對方在留言簿上寫上 Mr. 或 *Miss*，若只說「林打電話給你，要你馬上回電話給他」，可能會弄不清楚是「林××，還是林伯伯，…」等，英文則一定要用 *A telephone call from Miss*〔 **Mr.**, *Prof.*〕*Lin, please return her*〔 *his* 〕*call.* 就非常清楚了。

　　英語中用 *Mr.* 表示單身或結過婚的男人的總稱，用 *Mrs.* 表示已婚，*Miss* 表示未婚的女姓。近來女權運動者表示這是不公平的，美國最近也漸漸流行用 **Ms.** 表示女姓，其發音是〔miz〕。甚至在公文中都被承認了。但因在其他國家還未受到廣泛使用，初次聽到的人極可能會聽不懂。

怎樣表示道歉

　　美國是個講求效率的國家，任何可以用電話連絡的事都儘量用電話，所以並沒有相當於「對不起，用電話與您聯絡」的英文，如果您堅持表現禮貌或紳士風度，而用了 I am sorry to make a phone call to you.，對方一定會感到莫名其妙而反問你，Why？What's wrong with it？或 What on earth have you done？但如果本來應該當面說明，但卻用電話報告可說：

　　I should've come and seen you to tell the details, but I'm tied up these days.

如果是較不重要的人物，也可以說：

　　I wish I could meet you, but I have to stick to my desk today. So let me speak over the phone.

　　固然西方人很少爲打電話而未親自拜訪感到抱歉，但若在清晨或深夜打電話給別人，在東西方國家來看，都是不合理的。若是清晨打電話給別人時，可用：

I'm sorry to have called you this early, but....
　　（眞抱歉這麼早就打電話給你，但…。）

這種情形若發生於熟識的人之間，可說：

I hope I didn't wake you up.（希望我沒有吵醒你。）

極爲親近的人之間，則用

Did I wake you up?　等等表示歉意。

若是深夜打電話給別人時，可說：

I'm sorry to have called you this late, but....
　　（我很抱歉這麼晚了打電話給你，但…。）

　　雖然一般接到半夜兩、三點打電話來，又沒急事的情形，很多人都會氣得當場掛電話。萬一遇到這樣的情況，對方又若無其事地說：

Oh, are you still up?（喔，你還沒有睡啊？）

較有風度的回答應是不帶責備的口吻說：

No, no, I was dreaming a beautiful dream before
you disturbed it.（是的，還沒有。你打擾了我的好夢。）

「請問～在嗎？」

　　不論自己打電話到別人家裏或公司，問「請問～在嗎？」的時候，可直譯爲 **Is ～ in**？ in 是在， out 是不在，但打電話的一方不能問 **Is ～ out**？而當你說 **Is ～ in**？的時候，若發音短且低，外國人可能聽不懂，in 一定要發長音，且大聲。

　　Is ～ in？總是給人較不禮貌的感覺，所以最好記得用 **May I speak to ～**？ 或 **Can I speak to ～**？，或 **Can〔May〕I speak with ～**？的說法。

這種疑問句是禮貌的,譯成「請問某某人在不在?」

當然並不是所有場合都用禮貌的說法,譬如董事長用電話叫職員時,或對人有不滿的時候,可說 *I want to speak to ～*。

前述中提到,用 speak 的時候,介系詞可用 with 或 to,但用 to 的人較多。而 speak 很少用 talk 來取代。

「×××,你的電話」的說法

當對方請求通話的人是自己的同事,要通知同事「你的電話」時,最普通的說法就是 *It's for your.*,不必說 The telephone call is for you. 如果大家都豎著耳朵等待這是誰的電話時,只要作個手勢或使個眼色說 *For you.* 即可。這時只是補足動作上的不完全罷了。如果被找的人不在這間房間,而在別間辦公室時,或者這通電話是經過交換台,不能轉成內線時,你要說「請等一下,我去叫他來聽。」(*Hold the line, please. I'll get him to the phone.*),然後到隔壁去通知他有電話,這時你說「你的電話哦。」說 It's for you. 或 For you. 就不夠,要用完整的電話用語: *There's a call for you.* (有你的電話。)

或 *You're wanted on the telephone.* (有你的電話。)

在公共場合中叫人接電話,如集會會場、百貨公司、地下鐵車站或宴會等等,可說「～先生 (小姐、太太) 的電話,請至服務台接聽。」即

Mr.〔 Miss, Mrs. 〕～ is wanted on the phone. Please come to The Information Desk.

或 *There is a telephone call for Mr.〔 Miss, Mrs. 〕～.*

Please come to the Information Desk immediately.

被叫的人,可走向服務台,說:「我是～,剛剛聽到廣播叫我接聽電話。」即 *I am ～. I'm wanted on the phone.*

「他在接另一通電話」的說法

　　若是打電話來的人說要找 Mr. Smith，而 Mr. Smith 正在接辦公室裏另一通電話，這時可向打電話的人說 *Mr. Smith is on another line.* line 表「電話線」，~ is on the line 即是「來接電話」的意思。這在任何場合、人物的情形下，用法都相同。例如打越洋電話到芝加哥，接線生會說「芝加哥那方已經接聽了，請說話。」即

Chicago is on the line. Please go ahead.

如果是指名要 Mr. Scott 接的電話，接線生要說「史考特先生來接了。」即　*Mr. Scott is on the line.*

對方電話正在使用時，一般的慣用說法是：*The line is busy.*（講話中。），*There's cross-talk on the line.*（有人在講話。），*Hold the line, please.*（請稍待一會兒。）即拿著聽筒稍待一會兒的意思。

　　如果有需要記下的東西，而必須放下話筒去拿紙筆時，這時可說 *Just one moment.* 這只用於親人、朋友的交談，公事上則要說 *Hold the line, please.*。

「用電話聯絡」

　　聯絡的動詞是「 inform ＋人＋ of ＋事」，或「 communicate ＋事＋ to ＋人」，這兒的聯絡可用 call, ring, give ~ a ring, give ~ a telephone call 等等。

　　從前除了電話，其他的聯絡方式還有信、電報，甚至捎口信，但據報導顯示，近來無論個人或公司之間的連繫，信件和電報大減；相反的，電話通數卻增加了許多。日常生活會用到：「那麼，再聯絡。」（ *I'll contact you soon.* 或 *I'll get in touch with you in a few days.* ），現在都

要加上「用電話」（ by telephone ），這樣無論說者、聽者都會很自然
的接受。一般打電話常用的句子：

> *I hope you'll contact me as soon as you return.*
> *Can I reach you at this number?*
>   我可用這個電話號碼與你聯絡嗎？

> *"How did you reach Mr. Buskin?"*
> *"I called him at his office."*
> 「你是怎麼聯絡巴士金先生的？」
> 「我打電話到他的辦公室去。」

> *I'll have him get in touch with you.*
>   我會請他和你聯絡。

多加練習電話交談，也是增加字彙的一種方法。

電話訂約會

　　常常對方問我們「星期天是否有空？」我們就隨口答應了「有啊！」
但等到他說明了活動內容時，不想參加已經來不及，這種情況在日常生活
中常常發生。因此邀請對方的人，應該先把活動的內容告訴對方，譬如參
加這次野餐的有誰、吃些什麼東西，或者舞會是跳交際舞或其他，再看對
方是否決定參加。因此，不該劈頭就問 Are you free ~？而應該用以下
的問法：

> *Would you like to come?*
> *Won't you come with me?*《普通朋友之間的用法》
> *Why don't you come with me?*
>   《這句話口氣比較硬，稍微具有大男人主義的強迫用法。》

> *How about coming with me?*

類似這種說法不勝枚舉，以下列出比較通俗的一個例子：

Susie, I haven't gone anywhere for some time, and I'm thinking of driving to Sun Moon Lake this weekend, if it's fine. Would you like to come along with me?

（蘇西，最近我都沒有出去，這個週末如果天氣好的話，我想

　開車去日月潭，你願和我一塊去嗎？）

像這樣的應用實例非常多，但先要把基本句型練熟，以期能夠應用自如。

電話詢問

　　在電話洽商時，需要查筆記、檔案或通訊錄的情形頗多，例如問及飛機、火車的時刻表，其被詢問者應該說：

Just a moment, please. I'll check the timetable.

其原句型應為：「 check ＋被問及的事物＋ with ＋資料名」，但會話中將其簡化，還可將 check 改成 look up 這個片語：

Just a moment, please. *I'll look it up in the timetable.*

如果要「查某班飛機到達的時刻表」，則要說：

I'll look up the arrival time of the plane in the timetable.

　　英語中非常重視音節的強弱，只有音節的強弱才能產生節奏感，如上一句的 look up the arrival time of the plane 就應唸

　　look up the arrival time of the plane
　　　強弱　　　　強弱　強弱　　強

這種強弱交替的音律，是使得英語流暢的要素。若把 the arrival time of the plane 改用 it 代替，那麼重音自然就應該是 *look it up*〔強弱強〕。有些人常會說成 *look up it*，這種錯誤要特別注意。

　　言歸正傳，若告訴對方「我要查查看，請您稍候。」時，爲了省去重覆「您要查的事」，就用 it 來代替，可以用以下的說法：

look it up in directory （查通訊錄）
look it up in telephone directory （查電話簿）
look it up in the guidebook （查指南手册）
look it up in the annual （查年鑑）
look it up in the dictionary （查字典）

電話中讓對方久候時

　　電話打到一半，想要確定一下自己的時間許可否，就回到自己房間去拿備忘錄，找了一會兒，才想起是放在上衣口袋裏，於是又打開衣櫥，從上衣口袋中取出備忘錄，再回到電話邊，這中間大約花掉了 1～2 分鐘，像這類讓對方久候的情況下，當你再回到電話旁，該說：

I'm sorry to have kept you waiting （ *so long* ）.

或簡單地說：

Sorry to have kept you waiting.

再次回到電話邊，不需像中文說法一樣再說一次「 Hello 」，只要直接用（ *I am* ）*sorry*....

　　但是這用在非常親密的朋友或親人之間，就會給人生硬的感覺。相當於「久等了」的英文是：

Are you still there ?

回答者要說 *Yes, I am.*

　　我們認爲 Are you still there ? 是較合適的用法，但在翻譯時，不要譯「你還在那兒嗎？」，畢竟英文有英文的說法，中文有中文的說法，不必太牽強。

「請轉告對方有他的電話」

　　如果我們打電話去，而對方正巧不在，那麼就應該交代他的家人或同事，請他回電話給我們。若剛好接電話的是外國人，許多人就會亂了分寸，而說成：

　　Tell him I wanted to speak to him.
　　　　告訴他我有話對他說。
　或 *Remember I called.* 記得我打過電話。

這都是不對的。正確的回答是：
　　　（ *Please* ）*tell him* 〔 *her* 〕*that I called.*
　　　　　請告訴他（她），我打過電話。

或 *Will you tell him* 〔 *her* 〕*to call me back later*？
　　　請告訴他（她）稍候回電話給我好嗎？

其他「他知道你的電話號碼嗎？」「是的，他知道。」為：
　　　Does he 〔 *she* 〕*know your phone number*？
　　　Yes, he 〔 *she* 〕*does.*

但若不知道的時候，就得用如下的回答：
用自家電話的時候說：
　　　No, he 〔 *she* 〕*doesn't. My phone number is 700-0787.*
　　　It's my home number.

公司的電話則說：
　　　No, he 〔 *she* 〕*doesn't. My office number is 707-1413,*
　　　and extention 345.

在別處等候他的電話時，可用
　　　No, he 〔 *she* 〕*doesn't. The phone number is 331-4060.*
　　　It's the Hilton Hotel. He 〔 *She* 〕*can get me there.*

「電話不通」

在上班時間及假日的辦公室，或是全家外出的人家，打電話過去總是沒人接。當電話鈴連續響個不停時，英文稱之為：

There's no answer.* 或 *There wasn't any answer.

這時所用的現在式或過去式並無差異，其意為「接不通」。其次，將指電話的 It 改為一家人的 They 來使用才對：

They don't〔didn't〕answer.

以上的說法皆為英美人士的慣用法，除此之外，以下的各種用法，在意義上也通。

(***It***) ***looks like nobody's staying home.***
  好像沒有人在家。

(***It***) ***looks like everybody's out.***
  好像大家都出門了。

一般備有留言電話者，其使用的模式約為：「我們不在的時候，請利用留言電話」即

We have〔There's〕the answering service. So please leave a message when we're out.

「打電話」的說法

「打電話」的講法，大約不下二十種，依情況不同而各異，一般最常用動詞 call，正式禮貌的用法則為：give (one) a telephone call。以下是在中文上稍有差異的英文說法：

I'll call you. （我會打電話給你。）

Call me later. （待會兒打電話給我。）

Call me later, won't you ? （待會兒請打電話給我，好嗎？）

Give me a call tomorrow. 明天打電話給我。

Shall I give you a call later？
　我等一下打電話給你好嗎？

Ring me（up）at three. 三點給我電話。

Why don't you give me a ring？
　你何不打電話給我？

Why don't you ring me（up）tonight？
　今晚你打個電話給我好嗎？

I'll give you a ring soon. 我會儘快給你電話。

Buzz me any time.　隨時打電話給我。

Let's give him a buzz. 我們打個電話給他吧。

Shall we phone him（up）？　我們打電話給他好嗎？

I'd like to speak with you on the phone later.
　我想待會兒打電話和你說。

Did you call her（up）？　你打過電話給她嗎？

Do you mind my telephoning your place？
　我可以打電話到你那兒嗎？

When can I expect your telephone call, sir？
　你什麼時候才會打電話給我？先生。

I couldn't go through to you.
　你的電話老是打不通。

「掛斷電話」不是 cut the phone

　　「他說…，然後把電話掛斷。」，He said …, and cut the phone. 意為他因不高興，而用力把電話掛掉，不是普通的「掛電話」。相當「切」的英文不下三十個，但只要記得一句英文，「掛電話」的慣用法，就是 *hang up*。切忌說成 hang over（宿醉）。

若是在對方有重要會議或討論時，打電話給他，爲了表示歉意，可說：

I'm sorry to interrupt you in your meeting, but....

若對方仍是無法安下心來與你交談，你可說：

Am I disturbing your？ Maybe I'd better call you back later.

對方聽了這話可能會有兩種回答：

I'm sorry, but I.... （我很抱歉，但我…。）

或直接了當地回答：

Yes, you are.

電話號碼的讀法

英文的電話號碼和中文一樣，是一個數字一個數字唸出來的，如 1234：one two three four。若有重覆的數字可唸出兩個數字，或在數字前加 double，如 55：「five five」或「double five」。又如 453-5311：「four five three–five three one one」或「four five three five three double one」。「0」可唸成〔o〕或〔'zɪro〕。如 607：「six zero seven 或 six o seven」，但 zero 較 o 來得清楚。如 1040 唸成「one zero four zero」較「one o four o」來得清楚。因此，100 號應唸成「one zero zero」或「one hundred」。1000 則唸成「one thousand」。

其次，要懂得 the area code 是區城號碼，而 the local office number 則爲接於區域號碼之後的市區號碼。唸電話號碼時，要把分節號之前的三個數字唸一起，其餘四個數字再唸一起，分節號（-）不必唸出，如：

331-4060：

three three one, four o six o。

內線電話的說法

若在辦公室中有數線電話，除了後面一個或兩個數字不同，前面幾個數字都相同時，前面這幾個數字就稱為 *pilot number*。若一大公司的電話是 453-5311 到 20，不必將 pilot number 說出，只要說 *Telephones are from 453-5311 to 20*，印在名片上可用 453-5311/20 或 453-5311-20 即可。

在名片印製電話號碼時，可用縮寫 TEL. ——，Tel. ——，phone (s) ——。表示內線可用 EXT. 或 Ext. 區別。若又附上自宅電話時，可註明 Residence ～或 Res.～。

國際電信代表用語：

A	for Alfred	N	for Nancy
B	for Benjamin	O	for Oliver
C	for Charlie	P	for Peter
D	for David	Q	for Quebec
E	for Edward	R	for Robert
F	for Frank	S	for Samuel
G	for George	T	for Tommy
H	for Harry	U	for Uncle
I	for Isaac	V	for Victor
J	for Jack	W	for William
K	for King	Y	for Yellow
L	for London	Z	for Zebra
M	for Mary		

Subscriber Toll Dialing
國內長途電話區域號碼表

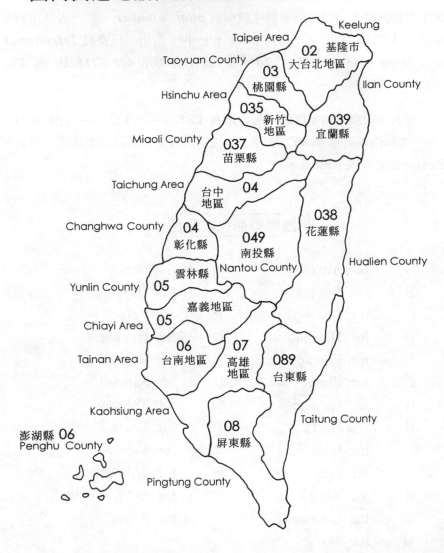

Keelung

Taipei Area

02 基隆市
大台北地區

Taoyuan County

03
桃園縣

Ilan County

Hsinchu Area

035
新竹
地區

039
宜蘭縣

Miaoli County

037
苗栗縣

Taichung Area

04
台中
地區

038
花蓮縣

Changhwa County

04
彰化縣

049
南投縣
Nantou County

Hualien County

雲林縣

Yunlin County

05

嘉義地區

Chiayi Area

05

06
台南地區

07
高雄
地區

089
台東縣

Tainan Area

Kaohsiung Area

08
屏東縣

Taitung County

澎湖縣 06
Penghu County

Pingtung County

第 **2** 章 **國內電話實況會話**

" Conversation for
Domestic Calls "

1. I'd like to speak to Mr. Johnson.

請詹森先生聽電話。

📞 對話精華

* I'd like to speak to Mr. Johnson. 請詹森先生聽電話。
* When do you expect him back？ 你想他什麼時候會回來？
* Shall I have him call you back？ 要我叫他回你電話嗎？
* I'll tell him as soon as he comes back.
  他一回來我就告訴他。

Dialogue

A： Hello！ *I'd like to speak to Mr. Johnson.*
喂！請詹森先生聽電話。

B： I'm sorry, but Mr. Johnson isn't here now.
對不起，詹森先生現在不在這裏。

A： When do you expect him back？
你想他什麼時候會回來？

B： I'm not sure, but he'll probably be back by three. Shall I have him call you back？
我不太確定，大概三點以前會回來。要我叫他回你電話嗎？

A： Yes, thanks. Tell him to call David Lin. My phone number is 321-4567.
好，謝謝。請他打給林大衛。我的電話號碼是 321-4567。

B： Okay, I'll tell him as soon as he comes back.
好的，他一回來我就告訴他。

📞 活用練習

1. I am sorry he isn't here now. 對不起他現在不在。

2. He is not in now. 他現在不在。

3. He is out. 他出去了。

4. Mr. Johnson is out now. 詹森先生出去了。

5. He's out for lunch. 他出去吃午飯。

【註】

I'd like to speak to ~　請~聽電話

expect〔ɪk'spɛkt〕*v.* 想；認為

probably〔'prɑbəblɪ〕*adv.* 大概；或許

have sb. + V　要某人做~

call sb. back　回某人電話

2. *Would you care to leave a message*?

你要不要留個話？

📞 **對話精華**

* *Would you care to* leave a message？ 你要不要留個話？
* *Would you ask him* to call me back？
　能不能請他回我電話？
* I'll give Mr. Wang your message *as soon as he comes back from lunch.*
　王先生吃完午飯回來，我會立刻把你的話告訴他。

Dialogue

A : Accounting Department. 會計部。

B : May I speak with Mr. Wang？
　　請王先生聽電話好嗎？

A : I'm sorry, he's just stepped out for lunch.
　　對不起，他剛出去吃午飯。

B : What time is he expected back？ 他什麼時候會回來？

A : Around one o'clock. Would you care to leave a message？
　　大約一點鐘。你要不要留個話。

B : Well, would you ask him to call me back？
　　嗯，能不能請他回我電話？

A : Certainly. Can I have your name and phone number？
　　當然。請問你的大名和電話號碼？

B : My name is David Lin and my number is 704-5525.
　　我叫林大衛，號碼是 704-5525。

A： Mr. David Lin at 704-5525. Thank you for calling. I'll give Mr. Wang your message as soon as he comes back from lunch.

704-5525 林大衛。謝謝你的電話。王先生吃完午飯回來，我會立刻把你的話告訴他。

📞 活用練習

1. He's just stepped out for lunch. 他剛出去吃午飯。

2. He's out for lunch. 他出去吃午飯。

3. He is not available right now. 他現在不方便。

4. He's in a meeting. 他在開會。

5. He's on another phone. 他在接另一通電話。

【註】

care〔kɛr〕*v.* 要；想

leave〔liv〕*v.* 留下

step out 外出

around〔ə'raund〕*prep.* 大約；將近（*= about*）

come back from ～ 從～回來

3. *Can I take a message*?

要不要留個話?

☎ 對話精華

* When *is he expected back*? 他什麼時候會回來?
* *May I speak to* Mr. Henderson?
  請找韓德生先生聽電話好嗎?
* Can I *take a message*? 要不要留個話?
* I*'ve got it*. 我知道了。

Dialogue

A: Hello! Is this Da-Da Company? 喂!是大大公司嗎?

B: Yes, it is, sir. 是的,先生。

A: May I speak to Mr. Henderson, manager of the Foreign Department?
   請找國外部經理韓德生先生聽電話好嗎?

B: I'm sorry, sir, but Mr. Henderson is out now.
   對不起,先生。韓德生先生出去了。

A: When is he expected back?
   他什麼時候會回來?

B: He'll be back at one o'clock. Can I take a message?
   他一點會回來。要不要留個話?

A: Thank you, but I'd rather have him call me back.
   謝謝你,不過我寧可要他回電話給我。

B: May I have your name, please? 請問您的大名?

A: Oh, my name is David Lin. Lin is my last name.
哦，我叫林大衛。姓林。

B: I see, Mr. Li. 知道了，李先生。

A: No, no, not Li, Lin … L-I-N. L for London, I for Isaac and N for Nancy.
不，不是李，是林。L-I-N。London 的 L，Isaac 的 I，Nancy 的 N。

B: I've got it — Mr. Lin? 我知道了—— 林先生對吧？

A: Right. 對了。

B: Does Mr. Henderson know your phone number?
韓德生先生知道你的電話號碼嗎？

A: Yes, he does. 是的，他知道。

B: All right, Mr. Lin. I'll tell him to call you back later.
好的，林先生。待會兒我會告訴他回你電話。

A: Thank you very much. 非常謝謝。

B: You're welcome. 不客氣。

(C) 活用練習

1. Can I take a message? （要不要留個話？）
2. May I take a message?
3. Would you like to leave a message?
4. Would you care to leave a message?

【註】

message〔'mɛsɪdʒ〕*n.* 留話；口信　　manager〔'mænɪdʒɚ〕*n.* 經理
foreign〔'fɔrɪn〕*adj.* 國外的　　***would rather*** 寧可
last name 姓（*first name* 名）

4. May I take a message?

要不要留個話？

📞 **對話精華**

* Ms. Yang speaking. 我是楊小姐。
* Mr. James is not in right now. 詹姆斯先生現在不在。
* *May I take a message?* 要不要留個話？
* Could you ask him *to call me at the Hilton Hotel, Room No.* 579? 你能不能請他打到希爾頓飯店579室來？

Dialogue

A : Public Relations office. Ms. Yang speaking.
公共關係部。我是楊小姐。

B : This is Brown—John Brown—from New York. I'd like to speak with your Director.
我是布朗—— 約翰・布朗—— 從紐約來的。請你們主管聽電話。

A : Mr. James is not in right now. May I take a message?
詹姆斯先生現在不在。要不要留個話？

B : Yes. Could you ask him to call me at the Hilton Hotel, Room No. 579? 好的。妳能不能請他打到希爾頓飯店579室來？

A : Certainly, Mr. Brown. Hilton Hotel, Room 579?
當然好，布朗先生。希爾頓飯店579室？

B : That's right. Thank you. 對的，謝謝你。

A : Thank you for calling. 謝謝你打來。

【註】

public relations 公共關係   director〔 dəˈrɛktə 〕*n.* 主管

5. *May I make an appointment call to ~* ?

我能約打電話給~嗎？

☎ 對話精華

* The number is 412-220-4433. 號碼是 412-220-4433。
* I'll *make the arrangement* with Mr. Lincoln.
  我會和林肯先生安排好。
* *You can reach me* at the Biltimore Hotel, Extension
  689. 你打比爾第摩飯店 689 號分機可以聯絡到我。

Dialogue

A : Hello ! Long Distance. 喂，長途電話台。

B : Hello. May I make an appointment call to Mr. James
Lincoln of Gettysburg, at 10 o'clock tomorrow morning ?
The number is 412-220-4433.
喂，我明早十點能約打電話給蓋茨堡的詹姆士・林肯先生嗎？號碼是
412-220-4433。

A : All right, I'll make the arrangement with Mr. Lincoln
at 412-220-4433. May I have your name and telephone
number, please ? 好的。我會和 412-220-4433 的林肯先生安排
好。請問您尊姓大名和電話號碼？

B : Yes, my name is David Lin, and you can reach me at
the Biltimore Hotel, Extension 689.
好的。我的名字是林大衛。你打比爾第摩飯店 689 號分機可以聯絡到我。

A : Thank you, Mr. Lin. 謝謝你，林先生。

【註】

make the arrangement 安排   extension〔ɪk'stɛnʃən〕*n.*（電話）分機

6. *Can you tell me what time he'll be in*?
請問他什麼時候會在?

📞 **對話精華**

* Can you tell me *what time he'll be in*?
  請問他什麼時候會在?
* When he comes in, I'll tell him *he had a call*.
  他進來時,我會告訴他有他的電話。

Dialogue

A : May I speak to Mr. Huang?
　　請黃先生聽電話好嗎?

B : I'm sorry, he is out now.
　　對不起,他出去了。

A : Can you tell me what time he'll be in?
　　請問他什麼時候會在?

B : Within half an hour, I think.
　　我想半小時之內吧。

A : I'll call him back in about thirty minutes then.
　　那麼我大約過三十分鐘後再打給他。

B : Thank you. When be comes in, I'll tell him he had a call.
　　謝謝你。他進來時,我會告訴他有他的電話。

A : Thank you. 謝謝你。

B : You're welcome. 不客氣。

☎ 活用練習

1. Thank you. 謝謝你。

2. Thank you very much. 非常謝謝。

3. Thanks. 謝了。

4. Thanks a lot. 多謝。

5. Thank you for calling. 謝謝你的電話。

【註】

be in 在～裏面；回來　　call〔kɔl〕*n.* 電話；通話
within〔wɪˈðɪn〕*prep.* 在～之內
then〔ðɛn〕*adv.* 那麼

7. *Sorry to have kept you waiting.*

抱歉讓你等候。

☎ 對話精華

* *Is this* Mr. Johnson's *home*? 是詹森先生家嗎？
* Why don't you *try to contact him* at his office? 你何不試著打到他辦公室找找看？
* *Hang on a moment.* 等一下，別掛斷。
* Sorry to *have kept you waiting.* 抱歉讓你等候。

Dialogue

A : Hello. 喂。

B : Hello, is this Mr. Harry Johnson's home?
喂，是哈利‧詹森家嗎？

A : Yes, it is, but he is out right now. Would you care to leave a message?
是的。不過他現在出去了。要不要留話？

B : Yes, but it's very urgent. 好的，不過這事很急。

A : Well, then, why don't you try to contact him at his office? I think he is there now.
嗯，那麼你何不試著打到他辦公室找找看？我想他現在在那裏。

B : Yes, I guess I could do that.
好的，我想我會試試看。

A : Would you like the number? 要不要號碼？

B : Yes, please. 好的，請說。

A : Hang on a moment, please. I'll get it for you.
　　請等一下，別掛斷。我去拿給你。

B : That would be very kind of you. 你人眞好。（非常感激。）

A : Just a moment. (*after a moment*) Sorry to have kept you waiting. If you phone 331-4060, you will get his office's switchboard.
　　稍等一會兒。（片刻後）抱歉讓你等候。你打 331-4060，那是他辦公室總機的電話。

B : 331-4060？　331-4060？

A : That's right. Then if you ask for extension number 35, you will get the Public Relations Division. You can reach Mr. Johnson there.
　　對。然後你請他轉 35 號分機，就會轉到公共關係部去。在那兒你可以找到詹森先生。

B : Thank you so much for your help.
　　非常謝謝你的幫忙。

A : You're welcome. Good-bye and good luck.
　　別客氣。再見，祝你好運。

【註】

keep sb. waiting 讓某人等候　　urgent (ˈɝdʒənt) *adj.* 緊急的
contact (kənˈtækt) *v.* 聯繫；接觸
switchboard (ˈswɪtʃˌbord) *n.* 電話總機
extension (ɪkˈstɛnʃən) *n.* （電話）分機
reach (ritʃ) *v.* 接觸；聯絡到　　division (dəˈvɪʒən) *n.* 部門

8. *Thank you for calling.*

謝謝你打來。

📞 **對話精華**

* Shall we have dinner together tomorrow evening?
   明天晚上我們一起吃晚飯好嗎?
* *Thank you for calling.* 謝謝你打來。

Dialogue

A: Shall we have dinner together tomorrow evening?
   明天晚上我們一起吃晚飯好嗎?

B: Yes, that would be nice, but I won't be free until six.
   好,那真好。不過我六點以後才有空。

A: That's all right. I'll pick you up at your office at six
   five. Is there any special place you'd like to go?
   沒關係。我六點五分來你辦公室接你。有什麼你特別想去的地方嗎?

B: No, you can surprise me. 沒有,隨你讓我驚訝好了。

A: OK, I'll do my best. See you tomorrow then.
   好,我會盡我所能。那麼明天見。

B: Thank you for calling. Good-bye.
   謝謝你打來。再見。

【註】

pick sb. up (用車)接載某人   surprise〔sə'praɪz〕*v.* 使驚訝

9. I'm sorry, he is on another line right now.

對不起，他現在在接另一通電話。

📞 **對話精華**

* He is **on another line right now.**
  他現在在接另一通電話。
* Will you **hold the line**, please？ 請稍候好嗎？
* I'm sorry to have **kept you waiting**. 對不起讓你等候。
* What can I do for you？ 有什麼事嗎？

Dialogue

A : Customer Service Department. May I help you？
顧客服務部，有什麼事嗎？

B : Yes, may I speak with Mr. Miller？
是的，可以請米勒先生聽電話嗎？

A : I'm, sorry, he is on another line right now. Will you hold the line, please？
對不起，他現在在接另一通電話。請稍候好嗎？

B : Yes, thank you. 好的，謝謝你。

(*a little later*)（片刻之後）

A : Hello. I'm sorry to have kept you waiting. This is Miller speaking. What can I do for you？
喂，對不起讓你久等了。我是米勒，有什麼事嗎？

B : Mr. Miller, this is David from Taipei. Long time no see.
米勒先生，我是台北來的大衛。好久不見。

10. *Who is calling, please*?
請問你是哪一位？

☎ **對話精華**

* *Who is calling*, please？ 請問你是哪一位？
* I'm sorry, but he is *on another line.*
  對不起，他在接另一通電話。
* Could you please *hold on a moment*？ Or will you
  call us back？
  能不能請你等一會兒？或是你要再打過來？

Dialogue

A : Hello. Is this 700-0787？ 喂，是 700-0787 嗎？
B : Yes, it is. 是的。

A : Please connect me with Mr. Huang.
  請黃先生聽電話。
B : Who is calling, please？ 請問你是哪一位？

A : This is Mr. John Park. 我是約翰・派克。
B : One moment, please. (*a moment later*) Hello, Mr.
  Park？ I'm sorry, but Mr. Huang is on another line.
  Could you please hold on a moment？ Or will you call
  us back？
  請稍候。（片刻之後）喂，派克先生嗎？對不起，黃先生在接另一
  通電話。能不能請你等一會兒，或是你要再打過來？

A： I'll hold the line. 我等一會兒。
　　(*one moment later*)（片刻之後）

B： Sorry to have kept you waiting. Mr. Huang is on the line.
　　Please go ahead.
　　抱歉讓您等候。黃先生來了，請講話。

A： Oh, thank you, Hello, Bob？
　　哦，謝謝你。喂，鮑伯嗎？

C： Oh, hello, Park. 哦，嗨，派克。

🕿 活用練習

1. One moment, please. 請稍候。

2. Hold the line, please. 請稍等。

3. Just a moment, please. 請等一下。

4. Wait a second, please. 請等一會兒。

5. I'll see if he is in. 我看看他在不在。

【註】

 be on another line 在接另一通電話
 go ahead （電話）請講話

11. What can I do for you?

有什麼事嗎？

📞 **對話精華**

* *How is the world treating you*? 你過得怎樣？

* *Just so so.* 馬馬虎虎。

* What can I do for you？ 有什麼事嗎？

* *Do you have time to come with me* to see the movie？ 你有沒有空跟我一起去看電影？

Dialogue

A： Hello, this is Sally. How are you, David？
　　哈囉，我是莎莉。你好嗎？大衛。

B： Couldn't be better. How is the world treating you？
　　好極了。你過得怎麼樣？

A： Just so so. What can I do for you？
　　馬馬虎虎啦。有什麼事嗎？

B： Well, I've go tickets for the preview of the American movie "The Big Country." It's at 1 o'clock this coming Friday. Do you have time to come with me to see the movie？
　　嗯，我買了美國片「大家園」預演的票。星期五一點開始演。你有沒有空跟我一起去看？

A： Great！I'll be happy to come. I've been pretty tied up
these days, but Friday is a good day for me.

　　好極了！我很樂意去。這些天我實在很忙，不過星期五我可以。

B： That's good. Let's meet at McDonald's at noon. I'll
buy you lunch.

　　那好。我們中午在麥當勞碰面。我請你吃午餐。

A： That's nice of you. 你真好。

B： Stay hungry. 午餐先別吃哦。

A： I sure will. 我會的。

【註】

　　treat〔trit〕*v.* 對待
　　(*It*) *Couldn't be better.* 好極了。
　　ticket〔'tɪkɪt〕*n.* 票；入場券
　　preview〔'pri,vju〕*n.* (戲劇、電影等的) 試演；試片
　　coming〔'kʌmɪŋ〕*adj.* 未來的；其次的
　　be tied up (工作) 忙碌
　　pretty〔'prɪtɪ〕*adv.* 相當地；十分地 (= *very*)
　　buy sb. lunch 請某人吃午飯
　　stay hungry 空著肚子不吃飯

12. *I want to invite you to a dinner party*.

我要邀請你參加晚宴。

☎ **對話精華**

* This is Bob. 我是鮑伯。

* I want to invite you to a dinner party tomorrow evening.
  我要邀請你明晚參加個晚宴。

* I'll *pick you up* at the hotel around 6:30 then.
  那麼六點半左右我來飯店接你。

Dialogue

A : Hello. John ? 喂，約翰嗎？

B : Yes ? 是的，你是哪位？

A : This is Bob.
　　我是鮑伯。

B : Bob who ? 鮑伯什麼？

A : Bob Lin. Frank Ford introduced me to you the day before yesterday. You remember ?
　　鮑伯・林。法蘭克・福特前天跟你介紹過我，記得嗎？

B : Ah, yes, now I remember, Mr. Lin.
　　哦，是的，現在我記起來了，林先生。

A： Just call me Bob. Listen, John, we're having a small get-together at my place tomorrow evening. You think you can join us?

　　叫我鮑伯就好了。明天晚上在我住的地方我們有個小小的聚會，你想你能參加嗎？

B： You speak too fast for me, Bob.

　　對我而言你說得太快了，鮑伯。

A： (*a little slowly*) I want to invite you to a dinner party tomorrow evening.

　　（慢了些）我要邀請你明晚參加個晚宴。

B： That's wonderful, Bob. Thank you very much.

　　好極了，鮑伯。非常謝謝你。

A： I'll pick you up at the hotel around 6：30 then. You wait for me at the front door. OK?

　　那麼我大概六點半來飯店接你。你在大門口等我，好嗎？

B： 6：30 at the front door? OK. Thank you again. Bye now.

　　六點半在大門口？好，再一次謝謝你。再見。

【註】

　　the day before yesterday 前天
　　pick up （開車）接載人
　　front door 前門

13. *What did he have to say*?

他要説什麼?

📞 **對話精華**

* Has there been any important mail, or phone calls for me ?
  有沒有我的重要郵件,或是電話?
* *What did he have to say ?*。
  他要說什麼?
* He wanted to *talk with you personally*.
  他要親自跟你談。

Dialogue

A : Has there been any important mail for me ?
   有沒有我的重要郵件?

B : No mail, sir. But there was a call this morning from David Lin.
   沒郵件,先生。不過今天早上有位林大衛先生打電話來。

A : What did he have to say ?
   他要說什麼?

B : He wanted to talk with you personally, so I gave him your home number.
   他要親自跟你談,所以我給他你家的電話號碼。

A : Well, the call hasn't come through, so I'll try to get him later. Oh, and before I forget, contact George Liu and arrange a meeting for tomorrow afternoon.

嗯，那通電話我還沒接到，待會兒我會試著聯絡他。哦，在我忘掉前先告訴你，聯絡一下劉喬治，安排明天下午的會議。

B : Yes, sir. Will that be all, sir ?

是的，先生。就那樣嗎？先生。

A : Yes, thank you. 是的，謝謝你。

【註】

　mail〔mel〕*n.* 郵件
　personally〔'pɝsn̩lɪ〕*adv.* 親自地
　come through （電話）接通
　contact〔kən'tækt〕*v.* 聯絡
　arrange〔ə'rendʒ〕*v.* 安排；籌備

14. *This is Mr. Lin speaking.*

我是林先生。

☎ 對話精華

* *This is he.* 我就是。
* *This is Mr. Lin speaking.* 我是林先生。

Dialogue

A : I'd like to speak to Mr. Yang.
請楊先生聽電話。

B : This is he speaking. 我就是。

A : Hello, this is Mr. Lin speaking. How are you?
喂，我是林先生。你好嗎？

B : Fine, thanks, Mr. Lin. How are you?
我很好，謝謝你，林先生。你好嗎？

A : Pretty good. 很好。

B : What can I do for you, Mr. Lin? 林先生，有什麼事嗎？

A : Well, I'm having several friends over for dinner this Friday, and I was wondering if you have the time to join us.
嗯，我有幾個朋友這個星期五要過來吃晚飯，我想知道你是不是有空來。

B : Sounds interesting. What time would you like me to come?
似乎很有趣。你要我什麼時候去？

A： Is six o'clock all right?
　　六點可以嗎？

B： That's fine. I think I can make it.
　　好，我想可以。

A： Very good. I'll see you Friday. Good-bye.
　　很好。星期五見。再見。

B： Thanks for calling. Good-bye.
　　謝謝你打電話來。再見。

【註】

　　pretty〔'prɪtɪ〕 *adv.* 很；相當地
　　over〔'ovɚ〕 *adv.* 過來；在那邊
　　wonder〔'wʌndɚ〕 *v.* 想知道
　　sound〔saʊnd〕 *v.* 聽起來；似乎
　　make it 可以；辦到

15. *I'd like to see you one of these days.*

這幾天內我想見你。

☎ **對話精華**

* I'd like to see you *one of these days*.
  這幾天內我想見你。
* I'll *be happy to meet you any time*.
  我隨時都很高興見你。
* *Suits me fine*. 對我很方便。

Dialogue

A : What can I do for you, John ?
約翰，有什麼事嗎？

B : Well, I'd like to see you one of these days. I'm leaving for Canada on a business trip soon.
嗯，這幾天內我想見你。我馬上就要到加拿大出差去了。

A : Oh, are you ? I didn't know that.
哦，是嗎？我不知道那件事。

B : Well, it was sort of sudden assignment.
嗯，是突然派我去。

A : How long will you be gone ?
你要去多久？

B : About two months.
大約兩個月吧。

A： That long? Well, I'll be happy to meet you any time
after six o'clock.
那麼久？好，六點以後我隨都很高興見你。

B： Good. How about tomorrow?
好。明天可以嗎？

A： That'll be fine. Where shall we meet?
可以。在哪裏見面？

B： How about the Hotel Flowers at 6:30?
六點半在華華飯店好嗎？

A： Suits me fine. 對我很方便。

B： All right. See you tomorrow, then.
好，那麼明天見。

A： Good-bye. 再見。

【註】

one of these days 這幾天內　　*leave for ~* 前往~
business trip 商務旅行　　*sort of* 有點~
sudden〔'sʌdn〕*adj.* 突然的
assignment〔ə'saɪnmənt〕*n.* 任命；指派
suit〔sut, sɪut〕*v.* 使方便；使適合　　then〔ðɛn〕*adv.* 那麼

16. *I'm afraid you have the wrong man.*
恐怕你找錯人了。

☎ **對話精華**

* *Are you sure that* you're calling George Lin ?
  你確定你找林喬治嗎？
* *I'm afraid* you *have* the wrong man.
  恐怕你找錯人了。

Dialogue

A : I'd like to speak to Mr. Lin. 請林先生聽電話。

B : Yes. This is Mr. Lin speaking. 是的，我就是。

A : Hello, Mr. Lin. This is Louis Liu.
嗨，林先生，我是劉路易。

B : Mr. Louis Liu ? 劉路易？

A : Yes. 是的。

B : Excuse me, but are you sure that you're calling
George Lin ?
對不起，不過你確定你找林喬治嗎？

A : Oh, no. I wanted to speak to Mr. David Lin.
哦，不是。我找林大衛。

B : Then I'm afraid you have the wrong man. The same
family name, but a different person.
那麼恐怕你找錯人了。同姓，但不同人。

A ： I'm terribly sorry.

非常抱歉。。

B ： That's all right. Do you have any idea which division he's working in ?

沒關係。你知道他在哪個部門工作嗎？

A ： I thought he belonged to the Computer Division.

我想他屬於電腦部門。

B ： All right. Just hold the line. I'll get you your party.

好的，請稍等一會兒。我替你找他。

A ： Thank you. 謝謝你。

【註】

be afraid (that) 恐怕　　sure (ʃʊr) adj. 確信的

wrong (rɔŋ) adj. 錯的　　family name 姓

different ('dɪfərənt) adj. 不同的

terribly ('tɛrəblɪ) adv. 非常地

division (də'vɪʒən) n. 部門　　belong to 屬於

party ('partɪ) n. (電話中) 通話者

17. *I'm sorry but no one by that name lives here.*

抱歉沒有叫那名字的人住在這裡。

☎ **對話精華**

* I'm sorry but *no one by that name lives here.*
  抱歉沒有叫那個名字的人住在這裏。

* That's our number all right, but *no Mr. Hatton lives here.*
  那是我們的號碼沒錯，不過沒有哈頓先生住這裏。

Dialogue

A : Hello. 喂。

B : Hello, may I please speak to George Hatton?
    喂，請喬治・哈頓聽電話好嗎？

A : To whom, did you say? 你說找誰？

B : George Hatton. 喬治・哈頓。

A : I'm sorry but no one by that name lives here.
    抱歉沒有叫那個名字的人住在這裏。
    What number are you calling? 你打幾號？

B : 700-0787. 700-0787。

A : That's our number all right, but no Mr. Hatton lives here. This is the Smith's residence.
    那是我們的號碼沒錯，不過沒有哈頓先生住在這裏，這是史密斯家。

B : Oh, I must have the wrong number. I'm terribly sorry.
    哦，我一定是打錯號碼了。非常抱歉。

A： That's all right. I hope you find Mr. Hatton. Good-bye.
　　沒關係。希望你找到哈頓先生。再見。

B： Good-bye and thank you.
　　再見，謝謝你。

☏ 活用練習

1. What number are you calling？ 你打幾號？

2. What's the name of the party you're calling？
　　你要找的人叫什麼名字？

3. What's the name of the person you want to speak
　　to？ 你找的人叫什麼名字？

【註】

all right 沒錯；沒關係
residence (ˈrɛzədəns) *n.* 家；住宅

18. *I'm sorry, but you have the wrong number.*
對不起,你打錯號碼了。

📟 **對話精華**

* Hello. May I speak with Miss Shelly Winters?
  喂,請雪莉・溫特斯小姐聽電話好嗎?

* Who do you want to talk to?
  你要找誰聽電話?

* I'm sorry, but *you have the wrong number.*
  對不起,你打錯號碼了。

* *I am terribly sorry.*
  非常抱歉。

Dialogue

A : Hello. May I speak with Miss Shelly Winters?
  喂,請雪莉・溫特斯小姐聽電話好嗎?

B : Who do you want to talk to?
  你要找誰聽電話?

A : Miss Shelly Winters.
  雪莉・溫特斯小姐。

B : I'm sorry, but you have the wrong number. We don't have anyone by that name here.
  對不起,你打錯號碼了。我們這裏沒有這個人。

A： Isn't this 700-0789 ? 這不是 700-0789 嗎。

B： No, it's 700-0787. 不是，是 700-0787。

A： Oh, I am terribly sorry. 哦，非常抱歉。

B： Oh, that's all right. 哦，沒關係。

【註】

We don't have anyone by that name. 「我們這裏沒有這個人。」注意
    by 的用法。 by the name of 是「名叫～」的意思。

terribly (ˈtɛrəblɪ) *adv.* 非常地

19. Can you send a cab to ~ ?

你能派輛計程車到～嗎？

📞 對話精華

* Can you *send a cab to the corner of Park Street and 10th Avenue* ?
  你能不能派輛計程車到公園街和第十街轉角處來？
* I'm from Taiwan. 我來自台灣。

Dialogue

A : Hello. 喂。

B : Hello. Min-min Cab. May I help you ?
  喂，明明計程車行。有什麼可效勞的嗎？

A : Yes, can you send a cab to the corner of Park Street and 10th Avenue ?
  是的。你們能不能派輛計程車到公園街和第十街轉角處來？

B : Yes, right away. Your name, please ?
  可以，立刻就去。請問您尊姓大名？

A : My name is David Lin and I'm from Taiwan. It's easy to find me.
  我叫林大衛，我來自台灣，很容易找到我。

B : OK, Mr. Lin. 好的，林先生。

【註】

cab (kæb) *n.* 計程車   avenue ('ævə,nju) *n.* 大道

20. You're just the person I wanted to see.

我就是要找你。

☎ **對話精華**

* You're just *the person I wanted to see.*
  我就是要找你。

* How about *dropping by my office* ?
  順便到我辦公室來如何？

Dialogue

A : Oh, hello, Ted. You're just the person I wanted to see.
哦，喂，泰德。我就是要找你。

B : Hello, Lin. What's on your mind ?
嗨，林。有什麼事嗎？

A : Well, I'd like to discuss a little business with you. I was going to call and see when you're free.
嗯，我想和你討論一些事情。我正要打電話看看你什麼時候有空。

B : How about dropping by my office tomorrow morning ? Say eleven o'clock ?
明早順道到我辦公室來如何？大約十一點鐘好嗎？

A : All right. Thanks a lot. I'll see you tomorrow, then.
好的。多謝了。那麼明天見。

B : Okay, so long. 好，再見。

A : So long. 再見。

21. May I speak with Mr. David Lin?

請找林大衛先生聽電話好嗎?

📞 **對話精華**

* ***Who's speaking***, please? 請問你是哪位?
* ***I wonder if*** I can drop by.
  我不知道是不是可以順道拜訪一下。
* ***Come over*** to the receptionist's desk and call me
  from there.
  來接待員櫃台打電話給我。

Dialogue

A: Hello. This is Min-Tai Trading Company.
    喂,明泰貿易公司。

B: May I speak with Mr. David Lin?
    請找林大衛先生聽電話好嗎?

A: Who's speaking, please? 請問你是哪位?

B: This is Sam Chou. 我是周山姆。

A: All right. I'll connect you. (*speaking to Dave*) Dave,
    here's a call for you from Mr. Chou.
    好的,我替你接。(對大衛說話)大衛,有位周先生找你。

D: Thanks. (*speaking into the phone*) Hello, this is Dave.
    謝謝。(對著電話說話)喂,我是大衛。

B: Oh, hello, Dave. How are you? 哦,嗨,大衛。你好嗎?

D: Fine, thanks. What's up? 好,謝謝。你好嗎?

B： I'm passing by your office. I wonder if I can drop by.
　　我正經過你的辦公室。我不知道是不是可以順道進去拜訪一下。

D： Sure. Where are you calling from？
　　當然。你在哪裏打的電話？

B： From the New Park. 在新公園。

D： Umhm. Come to the receptionist's desk and call me
　　from there. I'll get through in a few minutes.
　　嗯，來接待員櫃台打電話給我，我幾分鐘內就過來。

B： That's fine. I'll see you soon, then.
　　那好。那麼我們待會兒見。

D： Good-bye for now. 先再見囉。

【註】

connect（ kə'nɛkt ）v. 使連絡；使接通
What's up？ 發生了什麼事？；你好嗎？
pass by 經過　　wonder（'wʌndə ）v. 想知道
receptionist（ rɪ'sɛpʃənɪst ）n. 接待員
desk（ dɛsk ）n. 櫃台　　*get through* 過來；到達

22. *Could you tell me how to get to your office*?

請告訴我怎麼到你們辦公室好嗎?

📞 **對話精華**

* *I have an appointment to see Mr. Patterson* at 11 this morning.
  我和帕特森先生約好了今天早上十一點見面。
* Can you *get here by yourself*?
  你能自己到這裏來嗎?
* *You can't miss it.*
  你不會看不到的。

Dialogue

A: Hello. This is David Lin. I have an appointment to see Mr. Patterson at 11 this morning.

喂,我是林大衛。我和帕特森先生約好今天早上十一點見面。

B: Yes, Mr. Lin. He is expecting you at 11. Can you get here by yourself?

是的,林先生。他正等待你十一點來呢。你能自己到這裏來嗎?

A: No, I'm afraid not, and that's why I called. Could you tell me how to get to your office, please?

不,恐怕不行。這就是我為什麼打電話的原因。請告訴我怎麼到你們辦公室好嗎?

B： Surely. You are staying at Hilton now. Take No. 15 bus in front of the hotel, and get off at the Botanical Garden. Our office is right in front of the Garden. You can't miss it.

當然。你現在住在希爾頓飯店。在飯店前面搭十五號公車,在植物園下車。我們辦公室就在植物園前面,你不會看不到的。

A： Thank you very much. I'll see you soon.

非常謝謝你。我們待會兒見。

【註】

expect〔ɪk'spɛkt〕v. 等待
get off 下車
botanical〔bo'tænɪkḷ〕*adj.* 植物(學)的
miss〔mɪs〕v. 看不見;錯過

23. *I'm calling you from a bookstore.*

我是在一家書店打給你的。

📘 對話精華

* *Is this Mr. Johnson*？ 是詹森先生嗎？
* I'm *on my way* to visit you now, but I *lost my way*.
  我現在正在去拜訪你的途中，可是我迷路了。
* *Turn to the left (right)*. 向左（右）轉。

Dialogue

A： Hello. Is this Mr. Johnson？ This is Paul Brown speaking.
喂，是詹森先生嗎？我是保羅・布朗。

B： Hello, Mr. Brown. What can I do for you？
嗨，布朗先生。有什麼事嗎？

A： I'm on my way to visit you now, but I've lost my way.
我現在正在去拜訪你的途中，可是我迷路了。

B： That's too bad. Where are you now, Mr. Brown？
真糟糕。布朗先生，你現在在哪裏？

A： I don't know exactly. I think I'm somewhere on Lincoln Street. I'm calling you from a bookstore.
我不太確定。我想是在林肯街某處吧。我是在一家書店打給你的。

B： A bookstore on Lincoln Street？ It's at a corner, isn't it？ 林肯街的一家書店？那是在轉角處，不是嗎？

A： Yes, it is. And I can see a restaurant at the other corner.
是的。而且我可以看到在另一個角落有家餐館。

B： Now I'm almost sure where you are. You turned at the second corner. You should've turned at the first corner from the subway station.
現在我幾乎可以確定你在哪裏了。你是在第二個轉角處轉的彎。
你從地下鐵車站出來應該在第一個轉角處轉彎的。

A： Is that so? Then I'll go back to the first corner.
是那樣嗎？那麼我走回第一個轉角處。

B： It'll be better that way. You'll find a one-way traffic sign. That's where you have to turn to the left. Come up the slope to reach a six-story apartment house. My room is on the third floor.
最好那樣。你會看見一個單行道的交通號誌，那是你該左轉的地方。
走上斜坡來，到了一棟六層樓的公寓房子，我住的地方就在三樓。

A： I'm sure I won't have any trouble this time. Thanks.
我確定這次不會有任何問題了。謝謝。

B： I'll be waiting for you. 我等你。

【註】

on one's way 在途中　　*lose one's way* 迷路

exactly〔ɪgˈzæktlɪ〕*adv.* 確實地

bookstore〔ˈbʊkˌstor〕*n.* 書店

corner〔ˈkɔrnɚ〕*n.* 轉角處；角落

almost〔ˈɔlˌmost〕*adv.* 幾乎　　turn〔tɝn〕*v.* 轉彎

subway〔ˈsʌbˌwe〕*n.* 地下鐵路（火車）　　*traffic sign* 交通號誌

one-way〔ˈwʌnˈwe〕*adj.* 單向的　　slope〔slop〕*n.* 斜坡

24. *I recognized your voice right away.*

我馬上就認出你的聲音了。

📞 **對話精華**

* I *recognized your voice* right away.
  我馬上就認出你的聲音了。
* *It's so nice* to hear your voice again.
  再聽到你的聲音眞好。

Dialogue

A : Hello ! Is that you, John ?
  喂！約翰，是你嗎？

B : Who ? Philip ! Yes, this is John. I recognized your
  voice right away. What a pleasant surprise ! When did
  you get back to Chicago ?
  誰？菲立蒲！是，我是約翰。我馬上就認出你的聲音了。眞是愉快
  的驚喜！你什麼時候回芝加哥來的？

A : I just came back about a week ago. I tried to contact
  you by phone several times, but you were not in.
  我大約一星期前剛回來。我試著用電話連絡過你好幾次，不過你不
  在。

B : I'm sorry. I'm out most afternoons.
  對不起，我大部分下午都出去。

A : I'm glad I've finally caught you. And it's so nice to
hear your voice again.
很高興終於找到你了。再聽到你的聲音真好。

B : Welcome home, Philip.
菲立蒲，歡迎回家。

A : Thank you. 謝謝你。

【註】

recognize (ˈrɛkəɡˌnaɪz) v. 認出
right away 馬上
pleasant (ˈplɛzn̩t) *adj.* 愉快的
surprise (səˈpraɪz) *n.* 驚喜
contact (kənˈtækt) *v.* 與人聯繫
several (ˈsɛvərəl) *adj.* 好幾個

25. *What are you doing tonight*?

你今天晚上要做什麼？

📞 **對話精華**

* *What are you doing* tonight?
  你今天晚上要做什麼？
* I'd *drop over for a drink or two*.
  我順便到你那裏喝一兩杯。

Dialogue

A: Hi! What are you doing tonight?
喂！你今天晚上要做什麼？

B: Nothing. Why?
沒事。什麼事？

A: I thought I'd drop over for a drink or two. We haven't seen each other lately.
我想順便到你那裏喝一兩杯。最近我們彼此都沒見面。

B: O.K. That's a good idea. What time?
好，好主意。什麼時候？

A: How about nine?
九點好嗎？

B: That's kind of late. Why don't you make it a little earlier?
有點晚，你何不早一點？

A： All right. How about seven？
　　好，七點如何？

B： That suits me. Have dinner with us.
　　那可以。跟我們一塊兒吃晚飯。

A： Well, I didn't mean to invite myself over for dinner.
　　嗯，我沒有到你那兒吃晚飯的意思。

B： I know. I really want you to come.
　　我知道。我真的希望你來。

A： O.K. If you insist.
　　好吧。如果你堅持的話。

B： Good. We'll see you at seven.
　　好。我們七點見。

A： Bye. 再見。

【註】

drop over 順道拜訪　　*each other* 彼此
kind of 有點；有幾分
suit〔sɪut, sjut〕*v.* 適合
invite〔ɪn'vaɪt〕*v.* 邀請

26. *I'd like to make an appointment to see ~.*
我想約個時間見~。

📞 **對話精華**

* *May I ask who is calling,* please？ 請問是哪一位？
* *Let me check his schedule* now.
  現在讓我查一下他的時間表。
* *How about* tomorrow at noon？ 明天中午如何？

Dialogue

A： President's office. May I help you？
　　董事長辦公室。有什麼事嗎？

B： Hello. I'd like to make an appointment to see Mr. Frank Ford sometime this week, if possible.
　　喂，可能的話，我想這個星期約個時間見法蘭克‧福特先生。

A： May I ask who is calling, please？
　　請問是哪一位？

B： Oh, I am sorry. I am Mr. Kang Huang from Taipei, Taiwan. I've written to Mr. Ford several times.
　　哦，對不起。我是來自台灣台北的黃康，我寫信給福特先生好幾次了。

A： Yes, Mr. Huang. He's been waiting for your call this week. Let me check his schedule now.... How about tomorrow at noon？
　　是的，黃先生。他這星期一直在等你的電話。現在讓我查一下他的時間表…。明天中午如何？

B： Tomorrow at noon ? That'll be fine with me.
　　明天中午？那對我很適合。

A： We'll be looking forward to seeing you then. Good-bye,
　　Mr. Huang.
　　那麼我們期待您的光臨。再見，黃先生。

【註】

president〔'prɛzədənt〕n.（公司的）董事長
make an appointment 訂約
schedule〔'skɛdʒul〕n. 時間表
look forward to 期待

27. *I don't think I can make it by noon.*
我想我中午趕不上了。

📞 **對話精華**

* *I don't think I can make it* by noon.
  我想我中午趕不上了。

* That's too bad. 那真糟糕。

* I am terribly sorry and please *give my apologies to Mr. Ford.* 我非常抱歉，請替我向福特先生道歉。

Dialogue

A : Mr. Ford's office. May I help you?
　　福特先生辦公室，有什麼事嗎？

B : Hello. This is Huang, and I have an appointment to see Mr. Ford at noon.
　　喂，我姓黃，我約好了中午要見福特先生。

A : Oh, yes, Mr. Huang. You sound very much distressed. Something wrong?
　　哦，是的，黃先生。你似乎很苦惱。出了什麼事嗎？

B : Yes. I rented a car and started driving toward your company this morning, but somehow I ended up in the opposite side of the city. It's already 11:45 and I don't think I can make it by noon.
　　是呀！我今天早上租了車子，往你們公司開，不過不知怎樣，結果我竟然在城市相反的一邊。現在已經十一點四十五分了，我想我中午趕不上了。

A： Oh, that's too bad. It'll take at least one hour to get back into town.

哦，那眞糟糕。要回到城裏來至少要一個小時。

B： Is it all right if I come in that late?

我那麼晚到可以嗎？

A： I'm afraid not, because Mr. Ford has another appointment at 1:30. Mr. Huang, how about tomorrow afternoon?

恐怕不行，因爲福特先生一點半有另一個約會。黃先生，明天下午如何？

B： That's all right with me. I am terribly sorry and please give my apologies to Mr. Ford.

對我來說可以。我非常抱歉，請替我向福特先生道歉。

A： Sure, I will. Please drive carefully in a new town.

當然，我會的。在一個陌生的城裏駕駛請小心。

B： Thank you. Good-bye.

謝謝你，再見。

【註】

distress〔dɪ'strɛs〕v. 使苦惱　　start〔start〕v. 開始；發動

end up 結果；最後　　opposite〔'ɑpəzɪt〕adj. 相反的

make it 趕到（目的地）；成功　　terribly〔'tɛrəblɪ〕adv. 非常地

apology〔ə'pɑlədʒɪ〕n. 道歉　　new〔nju〕adj. 陌生的；新的

28. I'd like to see the doctor as soon as possible.

我想儘快看醫生。

📞 **對話精華**

* I have *a terrible toothache.* 我的牙痛得要命。
* I'd like to see the doctor *as soon as possible.*
  我想儘快看醫生。
* May I *make an appointment* now?
  我現在可以約時間嗎?
* *Dr. Yang's schedule is full* for today.
  楊醫師的時間表今天都滿了。
* See you tomorrow. 明天見。

Dialogue

A : Dr. Yang's office.
楊醫師診所。

B : Hello. I have a terrible toothache, and I'd like to see the doctor as soon as possible. May I make an appointment now?

喂,我的牙痛得要命,我想儘快看醫生。我現在可以約時間嗎?

A : Yes, but Dr. Yang's schedule is·full for today. How about 9:30 tomorrow morning?
可以。不過楊醫師的時間表今天都滿了。明天早上九點半如何?

B : That's fine. I think I can wait till then.
那好。我想我可以等到那時候。

A : May I have your name and address, please ?
　　請問您大名和住址 ?

B : The name is David Lin, and I'm staying at the May-
　　flower Hotel.
　　名字是林大衞，我正住在五月花飯店。

A : Thank you, Mr. Lin. See you tomorrow. Bye.
　　謝謝你，林先生。明天見，再見。

【註】

full〔fʊl〕*adj.* 滿的
mayflower〔'me,flaʊɚ〕*n.* 五月花

29. *I'm so glad I got hold of you at last.*

眞高興終於聯絡到你了。

📞 **對話精華**

* I'm so glad I *got hold of you* at last.
  眞高興終於聯絡到你了。

* Were you trying to *get in touch with me*?
  你一直試著和我連絡嗎?

Dialogue

A : The Foreign Correspondents' Club.
　　國外通訊記者俱樂部。

B : Hello, is Mr. Robert Wagner there?
　　喂,羅勃特‧華格納在那裏嗎?

A : Yes, he's right here. Just a moment, please.
　　是的,他就在這裏。請等一會兒。

C : Hello, Robert Wagner speaking.
　　喂,我是羅勃特‧華格納。

B : Hello, Bob? This is Lin speaking. I'm so glad I got hold of you at last!
　　喂,鮑伯嗎?我是林。眞高興終於聯絡到你了!

C : Were you trying to get in touch with me, Lin? If I'm not at home, you can usually reach me at the Press Club here.
　　林,你一直試著和我連絡嗎?如果我不在家,你通常可以在記者俱樂部裏找到我。

B: That's good to know. Listen, Bob, I've got news for you. 知道這樣眞好。聽我說，鮑伯，我有消息要告訴你。

C: What is it ? 是什麼？

B: My sister Susan Lin is coming back from Taiwan. 我姊姊林蘇珊要從台灣回來了。

C: That's great. When is she coming back ? 眞好。她什麼時候回來？

B: Next weekend. 下個週末。

C: Next week ? Okay. Let's get together tonight and plan a party for her. 下個星期？好，我們今晚聚一聚，計劃爲她開個宴會。

B: All right. I'll come to your place at 8. 好，我八點到你那裏。

C: Good. I'll be waiting for you. 好，我等你。

B: See you later. 待會兒見。

C: Good-bye and thanks for calling. 再見，謝謝你的電話。

【註】

foreign correspondent 國外通訊記者
get hold of （取得）聯絡　　*get together* 聚集
party ('partɪ) *n.* 宴會

30. May I use your telephone?

可以借用你的電話嗎？

☎ **對話精華**

* May I use your telephone？ 可以借用你的電話嗎？
* *I meant to say that.* 我是要說那個意思。
* Where would you like to call？ 你要打到哪兒去？
* *Please dial* 0 before dialing your hotel number.
  撥你的旅館號碼前先撥0。

Dialogue

A : May I borrow your telephone？
可以借用你的電話嗎？

B : I beg your pardon？ You cannot borrow my telephone,
but you can USE my phone.
對不起，你說什麼？你不能「借」我的電話，不過你可以「用」我
的電話。

A : Oh, yes, I meant to say that, but, you know, in Taiwan, we say " borrow a telephone."
哦，是的。我是要說那個意思。不過，你知道，在台灣我們說「借
電話」。

B : Oh, I see. I didn't know that. Now, where would you
like to call？
哦，我懂了。我不知道那樣。好啦，你要打到哪兒去？

A： I'm calling my hotel to find out if any important messages are in.

我要打到我旅館去查查看是否有重要的信息來到。

B： Then, please dial 0 before dialing your hotel number.

那麼，撥你旅館號碼前先撥 0。

A： Thank you.

謝謝你。

【註】

meant〔mɛnt〕*v.* 意欲（ mean 的過去式 ）
find out 查出
message〔'mɛsɪdʒ〕*n.* 信息
dial〔'daɪəl〕*v.* 撥（電話 ）

31. I'll give you the front desk.

我給你接櫃台。

📞 **對話精華**

* Just a moment, please. I'll *give you the front desk*.
  請稍候。我給你接櫃台。
* Mr. Miller *has checked out*.
  米勒先生已經結帳退房了。
* Did he *leave a forwarding address*?
  他有沒有留轉遞地址？

Dialogue

A : Hotel Flowers. 華華飯店。

B : May I speak to Mr. Miller, please?
    請米勒先生聽電話好嗎？

A : Do you know his room number?
    你知道他的房間號碼嗎？

B : I'm sorry I don't. 抱歉我不知道。

A : Just a moment, please. I'll give you the front desk.
    請稍候。我給你接櫃台。

C : Front desk. 櫃台。

A : Mr. Miller, please. 請米勒先生聽電話。

C：Just a moment, please. I'm sorry but Mr. Miller has checked out.
請等一會兒。抱歉，米勒先生已經結帳退房了。

A：Did he leave a forwarding address？
他有沒有留轉遞地址？

C：No. I'm sorry. He didn't.
對不起，沒有。

A：All right. Thank you. 好，謝謝你。

C：You're welcome. 不客氣。

【註】

give〔gɪv〕v. 替（某人）把電話接到～
front desk （飯店等的）櫃台
check out 結帳退房
forwarding（'fɔrwɝdɪŋ）*adj.* 轉遞的
address（ə'drɛs）*n.* 地址

32. *Do you know his room number, sir*？

你知道他的房間號碼嗎？先生。

📞 **對話精華**

* *May I speak to Mr. Jack Richards from New York*？
  請紐約來的傑克・理查茲聽電話好嗎？

* *I'll connect you to the front desk.*
  我給你接櫃台。

* I'm trying *to get in touch with Mr. Jack Richards.*
  我正試著和傑克・理查茲先生聯絡。

Dialogue

A : Hilton Hotel. May I help you？
希爾頓飯店，有什麼可以效勞的嗎？

B : Yes, may I speak to Mr. Jack Richards from New York？
是的，請紐約來的傑克・理查茲聽電話好嗎？

A : Do you know his room number, sir？
你知道他的房間號碼嗎？先生。

B : No, I don't.
不，我不知道。

A : Then I'll connect you to the front desk. Please hold on. 那麼我給你接櫃台。請稍候。

C : Front desk. May I help you？
櫃台。有什麼可以效勞的嗎？

B : Yes, I'm trying to get in touch with Mr. Jack Richards from New York, but I don't know his room number.

是的，我正試著和紐約來的傑克・理查茲先生聯絡，不過我不知道他的房間號碼。

C : Just a moment, sir.... Mr. Richards is in Room 987. I'll connect you right away.

請稍候，先生…。理查茲先生在987室。我馬上替你接。

【註】

connect 〔 kə'nɛkt 〕 v. 接通（電話）

get in touch with ~　和~聯絡

33. May I call on you at your hotel?

我可以到你的旅館拜訪你嗎？

☎ **對話精華**

* I have *a letter of introduction* to you from Mr. Johnson of New York.
  我有封紐約詹森先生給你的介紹信。
* May I *call on you* at your hotel?
  我可以到你的旅館拜訪你嗎？
* If you can't find me, *please page me*.
  要是找不到我，請叫服務生喊我。

Dialogue

A : Hello. I wish to speak to Mr. Palmer.
嗯，我想請帕爾瑪先生聽電話。

B : This is Mr. Palmer speaking.
我是帕爾瑪。

A : Oh, how do you do, Mr. Palmer? This is David Lin.
哦，你好，帕爾瑪先生。我是林大衛。

B : Why, hello, Mr. Lin. I'm glad you called me. I have a letter of introduction to you from Mr. Johnson of New York.
啊，嗨，林先生。很高興你打電話給我，我有封紐約詹森先生給你的介紹信。

A : Yes, I know. Mr. Johnson wrote me that you were coming to Taiwan. May I call on you at your hotel tomorrow ?

是的，我知道。詹森先生寫信給我，說你要到台灣來。我明天可以到你的旅館拜訪你嗎？

B : Please hold the line a moment. I have to look at my schedule. (*a few seconds later*) Yes, it's all right. Shall we say two in the afternoon ?

請稍等別掛，我得查看一下我的時間表。（片刻之後）是的，沒問題。我們就講好下午兩點好嗎？

A : Splendid. Then I'll be at your hotel at two.

好極了。那麼我兩點到你的旅館去。

B : All right. 好的。

A : What is your room number ? 你房間號碼幾號？

B : It's No. 302 on the third floor. But I'll be waiting for you in the lobby. If you can't find me, please page me.

三樓302號。不過我會在休息室等你。要是找不到我，請叫服務生喊我。

A : I'll do that, Mr. Palmer. See you tomorrow.

我會的，帕爾瑪先生。明天見。

B : Good-bye. 再見。

【註】

schedule〔'skɛdʒul〕*n.* 時間表　　***look at*** 查看
say〔se〕*v.* 講；說　　splendid〔'splɛndɪd〕*adj.* 極好的；絕佳的
lobby〔'labɪ〕*n.* 休息室
page〔pedʒ〕*v.* （旅館、俱樂部中要服務生）喊名找人

34. *Could we have a little talk over dinner tomorrow evening* ?

明天晚上我們可以吃頓晚餐稍微談一下嗎？

☎ **對話精華**

* Could we *have a little talk over dinner* tomorrow evening ? 明天晚上我們可以吃頓晚餐稍微談一下嗎？
* I'm glad to hear that.
  很高興聽到那樣。
* *That's fine with me.*
  那對我而言很好。
* *I am looking forward to* seeing you then.
  我期待著到時候與你見面。

Dialogue

A : This is Ms. Joan Pierce of the ABC Corporation. Mr. Lin, I have heard so much about you and your business from Mr. Frank Ford. I am very much interested in your business and I would like to hear more from you personally. Could we have a little talk over dinner tomorrow evening ?

我是 ABC 公司的瓊安・皮爾斯。林先生，我從法蘭克・福特先生那兒聽到很多關於你和你業務的事。我對你的業務很感興趣，我想親自聽你多講些。明天晚上我們可以吃頓晚餐稍微談一下嗎？

B : Thank you very much for your interest and invitation.
As a matter of fact, I also have heard about your company, and I was thinking of calling you tomorrow.
非常謝謝你的注意和邀請。事實上我也聽過你的公司，我正想明天
打電話給你呢。

A : I'm glad to hear that. May I pick you up about 7 at
the hotel ?
很高興聽到那樣。我大概 7 點到飯店接你好嗎？

B : That's fine with me. What should I wear ?
那對我而言很好。我該穿什麼呢？

A : Well, I'd like to take you to the finest restaurant in
this town. A coat and tie will be fine.
嗯，我想帶你到這城最好的餐館，最好穿西裝打領帶。

B : Thank you very much for your invitation. I am looking
forward to seeing you then. Good-bye.
非常謝謝你的邀請。我等待著到時候與你見面。再見。

A : Good-bye, Mr. Lin. 再見，林先生。

【註】

be interested in ～ 對～感興趣
interest ('ɪntrɪst) *n.* 興趣；關心
talk over 談論

35. *I'd like to order my lunch.*

我想點午餐。

📞 **對話精華**

* *I'd like to order lunch.* 我想點午餐。

* The lunch omelet is a little bigger than the morning one. *Would that be all right*?
  午餐的煎蛋捲比早上的要大一些，沒有關係吧？

Dialogue

A : Hello, Room Service.
   喂，房間服務部。

B : Hello, I'd like to order lunch.
   喂，我想點午餐。

A : All right, ma'am. 好的，夫人。

B : I'll have a tomato and lettuce salad, a tomato omelet....
   我要一份蕃茄萵苣沙拉，蕃茄煎蛋捲…。

A : Our omelet is served with a green vegetable.
   我們的煎蛋捲就附有一份青菜。

B : I'd like a salad, too.
   我還要一份沙拉。

A : Yes, ma'am. What kind of dressing?
   好的，夫人。要什麼調味料？

B : Oil and vinegar, please.
   油跟醋。

A : The lunch omelet is a little bigger than the morning one. Would that be all right, ma'am?

午餐的煎蛋捲比早上的要大一些，沒有關係吧，夫人？

B : Yes. 沒關係。

A : Do you want some rolls? 要不要小圓麵包？

B : Yes, and a pot of coffee, please. 好。還有請來壺咖啡。

A : All right, ma'am. Anything else?

好的，夫人，還要其他的嗎？

B : No, that's all. 不，就那樣了。

A : May I have your room number, please?

請問妳的房間號碼？

B : 311. 311 。

A : Thank you, ma'am. 謝謝你，夫人。

B : Thank you. 謝謝你。

【註】

room service （飯店等的）房間服務部

order（'ɔrdɚ）v. 點（菜）　　lettuce（'lɛtəs）n. 萵苣

salad（'sæləd）n. 沙拉　　omelet（'ɑmlɪt）n. 煎蛋捲

serve（sɜv）v. 供應　　vegetable（'vɛdʒətəbḷ）n. 蔬菜

dressing（'drɛsɪŋ）n. 調味料　　vinegar（'vɪnɪgɚ）n. 醋

roll（rol）n. 小圓麵包　　pot（pɑt）n. 壺

36. Hello. Can I order my breakfast for tomorrow morning?
喂，我能點明早的早餐嗎？

📞 對話精華

* Can I *order my breakfast for tomorrow morning*?
  我能點明早的早餐嗎？
* Can you *make it* at 7? 七點可以嗎？
* What would you like to have? 你要什麼？
* *Anything else*? 還要其他的嗎？
* That's all. 就那樣了。

Dialogue

A: Hello. Room Service. 喂，房間服務部。

B: Hello. Can I order my breakfast for tomorrow morning?
   喂。我能點明早的早餐嗎？

A: Yes, you can. What time would you like to have it, sir?
   是的，可以的。你什麼時候要？先生。

B: Can you make it at 7? 七點可以嗎？

A: All right, sir. What would you like to have?
   好的，先生。你要什麼？

B: Well, orange juice, bacon and eggs, toast, and a pot
   of coffee.
   嗯，柳橙汁，燻肉扣蛋，土司，和一壺咖啡。

A： All right. Anything else ?

　　好的，還要其他的嗎？

B： That's all. My room number is 234.

　　就那樣了。我房間號碼是 234。

A： Thank you, sir. 謝謝你，先生。

【註】

room service 房間服務（旅社等將食物、飲料等送到客房的服務。）

make it （口語）達成

bacon and eggs 燻肉扣蛋（煎的燻肉加上半熟的蛋，多當早餐。）

toast〔tost〕n. 土司；烤的麵包

pot〔pɑt〕n. 壺

37. *I'd like to reserve a table*.

我想預訂一張桌位。

📞 **對話精華**

* I'd like to *reserve a table for two on* Thursday, the thirteenth.

  我想預訂一張十三號，星期四，兩人的桌位。

* We'll be there *around seven-thirty*.

  我們大約七點半到。

* It's Smith, S-m-i-t-h, and *my first initial is G*.

  我是史密斯，S-m-i-t-h，我名字的開頭是 G 。

Dialogue

A : Asiaworld Plaza. May I help you ?

   環亞大飯店。我能效勞嗎？

B : Yes, I'd like to reserve a table for two on Thursday, the thirteenth. We'll be there around seven-thirty.

   是的。我想訂一張十三號，星期四，兩人的桌位。我們大約七點半到。

A : A table for two, on Thursday, the thirteenth. Just a moment. I'll check and see. Yes, there is one table for two available on that evening. May I have your name, sir ?

   十三號，星期四，兩人的桌位。請稍等，我查看看。有，那天晚上有張兩人的桌位。先生，請問您尊姓大名？

B : It's Smith, S-m-i-t-h, and my first initial is G.
　　我是史密斯，S-m-i-t-h，我名字的開頭是 G。

A : Thank you, Mr. Smith. We'll have the table ready for
　　you.
　　謝謝你，史密斯先生。我們會將桌位給您準備好。

B : Thank you very much.
　　非常謝謝。

【註】

　　reserve〔rɪˈzɝv〕v. 預訂（座位）
　　available〔əˈveləbḷ〕adj. 可獲得的
　　initial〔ɪˈnɪʃəl〕n.（姓名的）第一個字母

38. I'd like to reserve a room.

我想預訂個房間。

☎ **對話精華**

* *I'd like to reserve a room.* 我想預訂個房間。

* I want *a double room with bath* this coming Saturday and Sunday.
  這個星期六和星期天我要個有浴室的雙人房。

* We'll *have it ready* for you, sir.
  我們會替你預備好,先生。

Dialogue

A : Grand Hotel. 圓山飯店。
B : I'd like to reserve a room. 我想預訂個房間。

A : When do you want it, sir?
  什麼時候要?先生。
B : This weekend. 這個週末。

A : Thank you. Just a moment, please.
  謝謝你,請稍候。
C : Front desk, sir. 櫃台,先生。

B : I want a double room with bath this coming Saturday and Sunday.
  這個星期六和星期天我要個有浴室的雙人房。
C : Hold the line, please. 請稍候。

(a few seconds later) (片刻之後)

C： We'll have it ready for you, sir.
　　我們會替你預備好，先生。

B： Fine. 好。

C： May I have your name and phone number, sir ?
　　先生，請告訴我你的名字和電話號碼好嗎？

B： Yes, my name is....
　　好的，我的名字是…。

【註】

　reserve 〔 rɪˈzɜv 〕 *v.* 預訂
　double room （旅館等的）雙人房
　bath 〔 bæθ 〕 *n.* 浴室

39. I'd like to reserve a single room with bath.

我想預訂一間有浴室設備的單人房。

☎ 對話精華

* I'd like to *make a reservation*.
  我要預訂房間。
* I'd like to reserve *a single room with bath* for December 25th and 26th.
  我想預訂十二月二十五日和二十六日一間有浴室設備的單人房。
* I'll check and see. 我查看看。
* May I have your name? 告訴我名字好嗎?

Dialogue

A : Hello. 喂。

B : Hilton Hotel. May I help you, sir?
希爾頓飯店。我能效勞嗎?先生。

A : Yes, I'd like to make a reservation.
是的,我要預訂房間。

B : Thank you. I'll connect you with our reservation clerk.
謝謝你,我替你接我們的預約人員。

A : Thank you. 謝謝你。

C : Hello. May I help you?
喂,我能效勞嗎?

A : Yes, I'd like to reserve a single room with bath for December twenty-fifth and twenty-sixth.

是的,我想預訂十二月二十五日和二十六日一間有浴室設備的單人房。

C : Just a moment, sir. I'll check and see…. Yes, that can be arranged. May I have your name, please ?

等一下,先生。我查看看…。是的,可以安排,請告訴我名字好嗎?

A : Yes, my name is David Lin. D-a-v-i-d, L-i-n.

好的,我叫林大衛。D-a-v-i-d,L-i-n。

C : Thank you very much, Mr. Lin.

非常謝謝你,林先生。

【註】

reservation 〔ˌrɛzəˈveʃən〕 *n.* 預訂
connect A with B 連接(連絡)A 和 B
clerk 〔klɝk〕 *n.* 辦事員
single 〔ˈsɪŋḷ〕 *adj.* 一個的;單獨的
bath 〔bæθ〕 *n.* 浴室;沐浴
arrange 〔əˈrendʒ〕 *v.* 安排

40. *I'd like to cancel my reservation.*

我想取消預約。

☎ **對話精華**

* I'd like to *cancel my reservation*. 我想取消預約。
* Just a minute *while I check our records.*
  我查一下登記請等會兒。
* Thank you for calling. 謝謝你打來。

Dialogue

A : Ambassador Hotel. May I help you ?
   國賓飯店。我能效勞嗎？

B : Yes, I'd like to cancel my reservation and make a new
   reservation. My name is David Lin and I made a reservation for February tenth, but is it possible to
   change it to the twelfth ? With the heavy snow up
   here, my car broke down.
   是的，我想取消預約，訂個新的。我叫林大衛，我預約二月十日的，
   能不能改到十二日？這邊下大雪，我的車拋錨了。

A : Yes, just a minute while I check our records. Mr. Lin,
   it is possible to change it to the twelfth. Thank you
   for calling, Mr. Lin.
   好的，我查一下登記，請稍等。林先生，可以改到十二日。謝謝你
   打來，林先生。

B : Thank you. 謝謝你。

【註】

cancel〔ˈkænsḷ〕*v.* 取消　　*break down* （車子）拋錨；故障

41. *I'd like to confirm my reservation.*
我想確定我的預約。

📞 對話精華

* Just a minute. 請稍候。
* I'd like to *confirm my reservation*. 你想確定我的預約。
* *We'll be expecting you on January first.*
  我們期待你一月一日的光臨。

Dialogue

A : Benjamin Franklin Hotel. 班傑明‧富蘭克林飯店。
B : Reservations, please. 請接預訂部門。

A : Thank you. Just a minute, sir. 謝謝你。請稍候,先生。
C : Reservations. May I help you ? 預訂部門。我能效勞嗎?

B : Yes, I'd like to confirm my reservation. This is David
   Lin from Taipei, Taiwan. I've reserved a single room
   for January first and second.
   是的,我想確定我的預約。我是來自台灣台北的林大衛。我預訂了
   一月一日和二日的一間單人房。

C : Yes, Mr. Lin. We have your reservation from Taipei.
   We'll be expecting you on January first. Thank you for
   confirming your reservation.
   是的,林先生。我們接到了你從台北的預約。我們期待你一月一日
   的光臨。謝謝你確定預約。

【註】

confirm〔kən'fɜm〕v. 確定   expect〔ɪk'spɛkt〕v. 期待

42. *Will you please call me at* 6 : 30 *tomorrow*?

明天早上六點半請叫我好嗎?

📞 **對話精華**

* ***Will you please call me at*** 6:30 tomorrow morning?
  明天早上六點半請叫我好嗎?
* It's six-thirty. 六點半了。

Dialogue

A : Hello. May I help you? 喂,能為你效勞嗎?

B : Yes, operator. Will you please call me at 6:30 tomorrow morning?
是的,接線生。明天早上六點半請叫我好嗎?

A : Yes, sir. At 6:30 tomorrow. 好的,先生。明天六點半。

(*at* 6:30 *the following morning*)(第二天早上六點半)

A : Good morning, sir. It's six-thirty.
早安,先生,六點半了。

C : Thank you, operator. 謝謝你,接線生。

【註】

Will you ~ ?(表詢問對方意思)~好嗎? 〔用 Would you (please)
~ ?更客氣。〕

following (ˈfɑləwɪŋ) *adj.* 其次的;後面的

43. The lines seem to be crossed.

好像有外線干擾。

☎ 對話精華

* **The lines seem to be crossed.** 好像有外線干擾。
* I can't hear you very well. 我聽不太清楚。
* **Something is wrong with this connection.**
  這通電話有問題。
* May I call you back ? 我再打給你好嗎？

Dialogue

A : Hello. Is this Mr. Johnson's residence ?
    喂，是詹森先生家嗎？

B : Yes, it is. 是的，這裏是。

A : May I speak with Mr. Johnson ? This is David from
    Taipei. 請找詹森先生聽電話。我是台北的大衛。

B : Who ? The lines seem to be crossed. I can't hear you
    very well. 誰？好像有外線干擾，我聽不太清楚。

A : I can hear you all right, but something is wrong with
    this connection. May I call you back ?
    我聽得很清楚，不過這通電話有問題。我再打給你好嗎？

B : All right. That's better. 好，那會好些。

【註】
    residence (ˈrɛzədəns) n. 家；住宅
    cross (krɔs) v. （電話線路）干擾

44. *I can't hear you well.*
我聽不太清楚。

☎ **對話精華**

* *Is this the Lee residence*？ 是李公館嗎？

* Who's calling, please？ 請問是哪一位？

* Will you speak *a little louder*？
  你能不能說大聲一點？

* I am calling from the hotel lobby.
  我是在飯店的休息室裏打的。

* *I'll be waiting for your call*. 我等你的電話。

Dialogue

A： Hello. Is this the Lee residence？
　　喂，是李公館嗎？

B： Yes, it is. 是的，這裏是。

A： May I speak with Mrs. Lee, please？
　　請李太太聽電話好嗎？

B： Speaking. Who's calling, please？
　　我就是。請問是哪一位？

A： This is David from Taipei.
　　我是台北的大衛。

B： Who？ I can't hear you well. Will you speak a little
　　louder？
　　誰？我聽不太清楚。你能不能說大聲一點？

A: Oh, I'm sorry. I am calling from the hotel lobby, and it's noisy out here. I'll call you back from my room in two minutes.

哦，對不起。我是在飯店的休息室裏打的，這裏外面很吵。兩分鐘後我回房間打電話給你。

B: OK. I'll be waiting for your call. Bye.

好，我等你的電話，再見。

【註】

residence (ˈrɛzədəns) n. 住宅
Speaking. 我就是。
call back 再打電話來

45. *We were disconnected.*

我們的線被切斷了。

☎ **對話精華**

* I was talking to a party. *We were disconnected*.
  我正在跟對方講話。我們的線被切斷了。
* Just *hold the line*, please. 請等一下。
* Now *the line is connected*. Go ahead, please.
  現在線接通了,請講話。
* *The connection often goes dead* these days.
  最近線路常常斷掉。

Dialogue

A : (*banging on the receiver rest*) Operator ! Operator !
  (猛按聽筒架)總機!總機!

B : Can I help you ?
  我能幫忙嗎?

A : Yes. I was talking to a party. We were disconnected.
  是的,我正在和對方講話,我們的線被切斷了。

B : I'm sorry, sir. Just hold the line, please. (*a few seconds later*) Now the line is connected. Go ahead, please.
  對不起,先生。請等一下。(幾秒後)現在線接通了,請講話。

A : Thank you. Oh, Harry. This is David again. We were disconnected. I didn't hang up on you.
  謝謝你。哦,哈利,我是大衛,我們的線被切斷了。我沒有掛你的電話。

C：（ *laughing* ）I know you didn't, David.
（笑著）我知道你沒有，大衛。

A：I guess something's wrong with the switchboard or the phone lines here. The connection often goes dead these days.
我想是電話總機或是電話線有問題。最近線路常斷掉。

C：You'd better tell the chief of the Telephone Section.
你最好告訴電話部的主管。

A：I sure will. By the way, what were we talking about？
我一定會的。對了，我們剛才說到哪裏？

【註】

bang〔bæŋ〕v. 砰然作響　　　*receiver rest* 聽筒架
disconnect〔,dɪskə'nɛkt〕v. 切斷（電話）
hang up 掛斷（電話）　　switchboard〔'swɪtʃ,bord〕n. 電話總機
connection〔kə'nɛkʃən〕n.（電話的）連接
dead〔dɛd〕adj. 不通的；死的　　chief〔tʃif〕n. 主管；上司
by the way 對了；順便一提

46. *Do you give a discount*?
有沒有打折?

📞 **對話精華**

* Do you *give a discount* if we buy it in large quantities? 如果我們大量訂購,有沒有打折?
* *How many copies*? 要幾本?

Dialogue

A : Hello. I want to know the price of the large Webster's Dictionary.
喂,我想知道大本韋氏辭典一本多少錢。

B : Hold the line, please. I'll connect you with the Foreign Book Department.
請稍候別掛,我替你接外國圖書部門。

A : All right. 好的。

C : Foreign Book Department. 外國圖書部。

A : What is the price of the large Webster's Dictionary?
大本韋氏辭典一本多少錢?

C : It's $45, sir. 四十五元,先生。

A : Do you give a discount if we buy it in large quantities?
如果我們大量訂購,有沒有打折?

C : How many copies, sir?
要幾本,先生?

A： Oh, a dozen or two. 哦，一打或兩打。

C： In that case we can't give a discount, I'm sorry to say. Our rule is to give no rebate for the purchase of less than 50 copies at one time, sir.
　　對不起，那樣的話我們不能打折。我們規定一次買少於 50 本時不打折扣。

A： Well, we don't need that many now. Thank you just the same.
　　嗯，我們現在不需要那麼多。還是要謝謝你。

B： Thank you very much.
　　非常謝謝。

【註】

Webster〔'wɛbstɚ〕*n.* 韋伯斯特（ Noah Webster 美國辭典編輯家 ）
connect one with ~ （把電話 ）接到
give a discount 打折
quantity〔'kwɑntətɪ〕*n.* 數量
copy〔'kɑpɪ〕*n.* （書籍等 ）一本
dozen〔'dʌzn̩〕*n.* 一打
in that case 那樣的話
rebate〔rɪ'bet〕*n.* 折扣
purchase〔'pɝtʃəs〕*n.* 購買

47. *Where and when can I reserve seats*?

我到哪裏什麼時候可以訂到位子？

☎ 對話精華

* *Are advance tickets for "Star Wars" still available*?
  「星際大戰」的預售票還有嗎？

* All the tickets for that day *have been sold out*.
  那天所有的票都賣完了。

* Where and when can I *reserve seats*?
  我到哪裏什麼時候可以訂到位子？

Dialogue

A : Are advance tickets for "Star Wars" still available?
　　「星際大戰」的預售票還有嗎？

B : What date, sir?　幾月幾號的？先生。

A : The thirty-first of this month.
　　這個月三十一號。

B : Let me see... that's Saturday, isn't it? I'm sorry, all the tickets for that day have been sold out.
　　我看看…那是星期六，是不是？對不起，那天所有的票都賣完了。

A : That's too bad. How about the following Saturday, June 7?
　　眞糟糕。那再下個星期六，六月七號的呢？

B : Just a minute, sir. Yes, tickets are still available for June 7.
　　請等一下，先生。有的，六月七號的票還有。

A： Where and when can I reserve seats？
　　我到哪裏什麼時候可以訂到位子？

B： Please come and get tickets for reserved seats at this theater. Tickets are sold at the Advance Sales Window between 11：30 in the morning and 6：30 in the evening.
　　請來這家戲院拿預訂座位的票。早上十一點半到下午六點半在預售窗口售票。

A： All right. I'll be there around noon tomorrow.
　　好。我明天大概中午到那裏。

B： Thank you. 謝謝你。

【註】

　　advance ticket 預售票
　　available〔ə'veləbḷ〕*adj.* 可獲得的
　　date〔det〕*n.* 日期
　　sell out 售完
　　advance sales window 預售窗口
　　around〔ə'raʊnd〕*prep.* 大約

48. Do you have a reserved seat for tomorrow evening?

你們有沒有明天晚上的預約座位?

📞 **對話精華**

* ***Do you have a reserved seat for tomorrow evening?***
  你們有沒有明天晚上的預約座位?
* ***Thank you for your information.***
  謝謝你提供的消息。

Dialogue

A : Hoover Theater. May I help you?
   豪華戲院。我能爲你效勞嗎?

B : Yes, I would like to reserve a seat for your current show. Do you have a reserved seat for tomorrow evening?
   是的,我想預訂你們目前的表演的座位。你們有沒有沒明天晚上的預約座位?

A : No, sir. Tomorrow's seats are all sold out. You might ask a ticket broker.
   沒有了,先生。明天的座位全賣完了。你可以問問戲票經紀人。

B : What? A ticket broker? Where can I find him?
   什麼?戲票經紀人?我可以在什麼地方找到他?

A : There is usually one around your hotel. You can ask one of the bellboys.
   通常在你的飯店附近就有。你可以問問服務生。

B : By the way, what time does the show begin ?
　　順便一提，表演什麼時候開始？

A : It begins at 7 p.m., sir.
　　晚上七點鐘開始，先生。

B : Thank you for your information.
　　謝謝你提供的消息。

【註】

current〔'kɜ·ənt〕*adj.* 現今的；目前的
show〔ʃo〕*n.* 表演
sell out 賣完
broker〔'brokɚ〕*n.* 經紀人；掮客
bellboy〔'bɛl,bɔɪ〕*n.*（旅館、俱樂部等）男服務生

49. Put one dollar eighty cents in the coin slot.

把一元八角投入投幣口。

📞 **對話精華**

* * *I'm trying to call New York.*
  我要打到紐約。

* * Will you please *put one dollar eighty cents in the coin slot* ?
  請你在投幣口投入一元八角好嗎？

* * You can put in that amount *in any combination*.
  那數目你怎樣的組合放進去都可以。

* * Now you can *dial the number* in New York.
  現在你可以撥紐約的號碼了。

Dialogue

A : Long Distance. May I help you ?
   長途電話台。有什麼可以效勞的嗎？

B : Yes, operator. I'm trying to call New York.
   是的，接線生。我要打到紐約。

A : Will you please put one dollar eighty cents in the coin slot ?
   請你在投幣口投入一元八角好嗎？

B : One dollar eighty cents ?
   一元八角？

A : Yes, you see the coin slot ? You can put in that amount in any combination, sir.

是的，你看見投幣口了嗎？那數目你怎樣的組合放進去都可以，先生。

B : Let me see... six quarters and 3 dimes....

我看看…六個二角五分和三個一角…。

A : Thank you, sir. Now you can dial the number in New York. You can speak for three minutes, sir.

謝謝你，先生。現在你可以撥紐約的號碼了。你可以說三分鐘，先生。

【註】

coin slot （公共電話的）投幣口
amount〔ə'maʊnt〕 *n.* 總數
combination〔,kɑmbə'neʃən〕 *n.* 組合
quarter〔'kwɔrtɚ〕 *n.* 二角五分的錢幣
dime〔daɪm〕 *n.* 一角的錢幣

50. *I'm in Room 776, and my name is David Lin.*

我住 776 室，我的名字是林大衛。

☎ 對話精華

* I'd like to place *person-to-person call*.
  我想打通叫人電話。
* That's correct. 對的。
* This is Mr. Frank Hamilton speaking.
  我是法蘭克‧漢密爾頓。
* *Go ahead.* 請講。
* Your party is *on the line* now. 對方來接了。

Dialogue

A : Long Distance. 長途電話台。

B : Operator, I'd like to place a person-to-person call to a Frank Hamilton in Fairfax, Virginia. The number is Area Code 703-543-2741.
   接線生，我想打通叫人電話到維吉尼亞的費爾費克思找位法蘭克‧漢密爾頓先生。電話號碼是區域號 703-543-2741 。

A : That's 703-543-2741, Frank Hamilton.
   703-543-2741 ，法蘭克‧漢密爾頓先生。

B : That's correct.
   對的。

A : Your room number and your name, please.
　　請問您房間號碼和尊姓大名。

B : I'm in Room 776, and my name is David Lin.
　　我住 776 室，我的名字是林大衛。

A : Thank you, Mr. Lin. Hold the line, please. I'll connect you to the number.
　　謝謝你，林先生。請稍候。我替你接那個號碼。

　　(*Operator calls Mr. Frank Hamilton's number.*)
　　（接線生撥法蘭克‧漢密爾頓的號碼。）

C : Hello ? 喂？

A : Hello. Long distance calling for Mr. Frank Hamilton.
　　喂。長途電話找法蘭克‧漢密爾頓先生。

C : Yes, this is Mr. Frank Hamilton speaking.
　　是的，我是法蘭克‧漢密爾頓。

A : (*to Mr. Lin*) Go ahead, Mr. Lin. Your party is on the line now.
　　（對林先生）請講，林先生。對方來接了。

【註】

Virginia〔vəˈdʒɪnjə〕*n.* 維吉尼亞州（美國東部的一州）

area〔ˈɛrɪə〕*n.* 區域

code〔kod〕*n.* 號碼；密碼

51. *Sorry to disturb you so late at night.*
抱歉晚上這麼晚了還打擾你們。

📞 **對話精華**

* ***I'm terribly sorry*** to disturb you so late at night.
  真抱歉晚上這麼晚了還打擾你們。
* I have ***some urgent business with Mr. Brown.***
  我有很緊急的事找布朗先生。
* I am sorry ***to call you up so late.***
  對不起那麼晚打電話給你。

Dialogue

A : Is this Mr. Frank Brown's residence ?
   是法蘭克・布朗公館嗎？

B : Yes, it is. 是的。

A : I'm terribly sorry to disturb you so late at night, but
   I have some urgent business with Mr. Brown. My name
   is David. Is Mr. Brown in, please ?
   非常抱歉晚上這麼晚了還打擾你們，不過我有很緊急的事找布朗先
   生。我叫大衛。請問布朗先生在嗎？

B : Just a minute. I'll call him.
   等一下，我去叫他。

   —— Dad, it's for you. 爸，你的電話。

   (*Dad's Coming.*) (爸爸來了。)

C： Brown speaking.

　　我是布朗。

A： Mr. Brown, this is David. I'm sorry to call you up so late, but I have to....

　　布朗先生，我是大衛。對不起那麼晚打電話給你，但是我必須…。

【註】

　　residence ('rɛzədəns) *n.* 公館；住宅

　　disturb (dɪ'stɚb) *v.* 打擾

　　urgent ('ɝdʒənt) *adj.* 緊急的

　　call up 打電話

52. *I'm sorry that I couldn't return your call last night.*

對不起，我昨晚沒辦法回你的電話。

☎ **對話精華**

* I'm sorry that *I couldn't return your call last night.*
  對不起，我昨晚沒辦法回你的電話。
* *I got your message* right now.
  我現在知道你留的話了。
* It's too late. 太晚了。

Dialogue

A : Hello, Bill. This is John.
   喂，比爾，我是約翰。

B : Oh, hi, John. 哦，嗨，約翰。

A : I'm sorry that I couldn't return your call last night. I was out at my friend's house, and they asked me to stay over. I got your message right now.
   對不起我昨晚無法回你電話。我到我朋友家去了，他們要我過夜。我現在知道你留的話了。

B : It's too late, John. We had a big barbecue party last night, and I wanted to ask you to come.
   太遲了，約翰。我們昨晚有個盛大的烤肉宴會，我本想請你來的。

A : That's too bad. I hope I can join you next time.
   真可惜。希望下次能加入你們。

B : Well, next time I'll be sure to get in touch with you
　　earlier. Thank you for calling.
　　嗯，下次我一定早點跟你聯絡。謝謝你打來。

A : Thank you, Bill. Goodbye.
　　謝謝你，比爾。再見。

【註】

stay over 過夜
barbecue (ˈbɑrbɪ͵kju) *n.* 烤肉
get in touch with ~ 和~聯絡

53. *Would you like to reserve a copy*?
你要不要預訂一本？

📞 **對話精華**

* Would you like to *reserve a copy*?
  你要不要預訂一本？
* I'm sorry, but I can't hear you very well. *Would you mind speaking a little louder*?
  對不起，我聽不太清楚。你能不能說大聲一點？

Dialogue

A : This is the Penguin Bookstore. May I help you?
   這裏是企鵝書店。要我爲你效勞嗎？

B : Yes. Have you got the American monthly magazine, "Harpers"?
   是的。你們有沒有美國月刊雜誌「Harpers」？

A : What month, sir? 哪個月的？先生。

B : This month's. 這個月的。

A : Just a moment, please. (*a few seconds later*) Yes, we have a few copies left, but they're going very fast. Would you like to reserve a copy?
   請稍候。（ 片刻之後 ）有的，我們留有幾本，不過賣得很快。你要不要預訂一本？

B : Yes, please. 好的。

A : May I have your name, sir?
   先生，請問尊姓大名？

B : Yes. My name is David Lin. 哦，我叫林大衛。

A : I'm sorry, but I can't hear you very well. Would you mind speaking a little louder ?
對不起，我聽不清楚。你能不能說大聲一點？

B : (*louder*) David Lin.
（大聲些）林大衛。

A : Mr. David Lin ? 林大衛先生？

B : That's right. 對。

A : When will you come down for it, Mr. Lin ?
你什麼時候會來拿？林先生。

B : I'll come right down for it.
我馬上去拿。

A : Thank you. We'll be waiting for you, Mr. Lin.
謝謝你。我們等你，林先生。

【註】

penguin〔'pɛŋgwɪn〕*n.* 企鵝

bookstore〔'bʊk,stor〕*n.* 書店

monthly〔'mʌnθlɪ〕*adj.* 每月一次的

magazine〔,mægə'zin〕*n.* 雜誌

harper〔'hɑrpɚ〕*n.* 豎琴師（此為雜誌名）

left〔lɛft〕*v.* 留下（leave 的過去分詞）

go〔go〕*v.* 賣；銷售

come down 過來

right〔raɪt〕*adv.* 馬上；即刻

54. The cups haven't been delivered yet.
杯子還沒送過來。

📞 **對話精華**

* I bought a dozen tea cups a week ago. But *the cups haven't been delivered yet*.
  我一個星期前買了一打茶杯，但是杯子還沒送過來。
* I'll *check it and call you back* in ten minutes.
  我會查一下，過十分鐘後回電給你。

Dialogue

A : This is the Chinaware Department.
瓷器部。

B : This is Mrs. Lin of Manhattan. I bought a dozen tea cups a week ago. But the cups haven't been delivered yet. I'm expecting a few guests next Sunday and I'll have to use them.
我是曼哈坦的林太太。我一個星期前買了一打茶杯，但是杯子還沒送過來。我下星期天會有些客人來，要用杯子。

A : I'm sorry, ma'am. I'll check it immediately. Can I have your full name, address and phone number?
對不起，夫人。我馬上查看看。可以請問你的全名，住址和電話號碼嗎？

B : Yes. This is Mrs. Lin, Nancy Lin. My address is 1-2-3 Broadway, Manhattan, and the phone number is 331-4060.
好的。我是林太太，林南施。我的住址是曼哈坦，百老匯 1-2-3 號，電話號碼是 331-4060。

A： Thank you, ma'am. I'll check it with Delivery Department and call you back in ten or fifteen minutes.
謝謝你，夫人。我會查一下遞送部門，十或十五分鐘後會回電給你。

B： All right. I'll be waiting for your call.
好。我等你的電話。

A： Thank you, ma'am.
謝謝你，夫人。

【註】

chinaware (ˈtʃaɪnəˌwɛr) *n.* 瓷器
Manhattan (mænˈhætn) *n.* 曼哈坦（紐約市內之島嶼，爲該市主要之一區）
deliver (dɪˈlɪvɚ) *v.* 遞送
expect (ɪkˈspɛkt) *v.* 期待
guest (gɛst) *n.* 客人
delivery (dɪˈlɪvərɪ) *n.* 遞送
call sb. back 回電話給某人

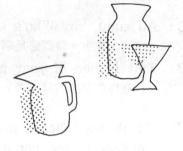

55. *I hope you'll be careful hereafter.*

希望你們以後小心一點。

📞 **對話精華**

* I'll **call him to the phone.** 我請他聽電話。
* *I hope* you'll be careful hereafter.
  希望你們以後小心一點。
* *We won't let it happen again.*
  我們不會再讓這種事發生。

Dialogue

A : This is the New York Times. 這裏是紐約時報。
B : Sales Department, please. 請接門市部。

C : This is the Sales Department.
   這裏是門市部。
B : I want to speak to the sales manager.
   我找門市部經理聽電話。

C : All right, sir. Who's speaking, please ?
   好的，先生。請問您是哪一位？
B : This is one of your newspaper subscribers.
   我是你們報紙的訂閱者。

C : Thank you. Please hold the line, I'll call the sales
   manager to the phone.
   謝謝你，請不要掛斷，我請門市部經理聽電話。

(*a few seconds later*) (片刻之後)

D : This is John Brown, sales manager. What can I do for you, sir ?

我是門市部經理約翰・布朗。有什麼事嗎？先生。

B : My name is David Lin. I applied for a subscription to your newspaper a few days ago. But I haven't received the paper yet. When can you get the paper delivered ?

我叫林大衛。我幾天前申請了訂閱你們報紙，但是還沒收到。你們什麼時候會把報紙送來？

D : Oh, I'm terribly sorry. There must've been something wrong at our end. I'll send directions to the sales agency for your area immediately and get the papers delivered to your house without fail tomorrow. We'll also have the papers of the past few days together tomorrow. Will you kindly wait until tomorrow ?

哦，非常抱歉。一定是我們的錯。我立刻傳送指示到你們那區的經銷處去，明天必定把報紙送到你家去。我們會把過去幾天的報紙連同明天的一起送去。請你等到明天好嗎？

B : All right. I hope you'll be careful hereafter.

好。希望你們以後小心一點。

D : Yes, we will. We won't let it happen again.

好的，我們會的。我們不會再讓這種事發生。

B : Good. 很好。

D : Thank you, Mr. Lin. Thank you very much.

謝謝你，林先生。非常謝謝。

【註】

subscriber〔səb'skraɪbɚ〕n. 訂閱者　*apply for* 申請

agency〔'edʒənsɪ〕n. 經銷處

without fail 必定；無誤

56. *I want to check if my account has received the remittance from* ～.

我想查一下～的匯款是否已經匯入我的帳戶裏。

☎ **對話精華**

* *Connect me with the savings accounts section*, please.
  請替我接儲蓄存款部。

* *I want to check* if my account has received the remittance from Lin.
  我想查一下林先生的匯款是否已經匯入我的帳戶裏。

* A total of $1,500 *has been remitted to your account*.
  一筆總共一千五百元的款項已經匯入你的戶頭了。

Dialogue

A : This is the Bank of America.
   這裏是美國銀行。

B : Connect me with the Savings Accounts Section, please.
   請替我接儲蓄存款部。

C : May I help you, sir ?
   要我爲您效勞嗎？先生。

B : I want to check if my account has received the re-mittance from Taipei Trading Corporation in New York.
   我想查一下紐約的台北貿易公司的匯款，是否已經匯入我的帳戶。

C : May I has your name and account book number ?
   請問大名和帳簿號碼？

B : Paul Brown. The number is 054-1205708.
保羅・布朗。帳號是 054-1205708。

C : 054-1205708 ?

B : Right. 對的。

(*a little while later*) (片刻之後)

C : I'm sorry to have kept you waiting. A total of $1,500 has been remitted to your account.
對不起，讓您久等了。一筆總共一千五百元的款項已經匯入你的戶頭了。

B : All right, thank you. 好的，謝謝你。
C : Thank you very much. 非常謝謝。

【註】

savings account 儲蓄存款帳戶
remittance (rɪ'mɪtn̩s) *n.* 匯款
trading ('tredɪŋ) *adj.* 貿易的
corporation (‚kɔrpə'reʃən) *n.* 公司
account book 帳簿
total ('totl̩) *n.* 總共
account (ə'kaunt) *n.* 戶頭；帳戶

57. *I'm sorry, but Mr. Lin's gone on a trip.*
抱歉，林先生旅行去了。

☎ 對話精華

* I'm sorry, but *Mr. Lin's gone on a trip.*
  抱歉，林先生旅行去了。

* When will he return? 他什麼時候回來？

* *He'll be back* next Monday.
  他下星期一會回來。

Dialogue

A: May I speak to Mr. Lin?
　　請林先生聽電話好嗎？

B: Which Lin, sir? There are two Lins here.
　　那位林先生？先生。這裏有兩位林先生。

A: Oh? Mr. Lin who is head of the Export Section.
　　哦？是外國銷部主管林先生。

B: Oh, the chief? That's Mr. David Lin, then.
　　哦，主管？那麼是林大衛先生。

A: That's right. 對了。

B: I'm sorry, but Mr. Lin's gone on a trip.
　　抱歉，林先生旅行去了。

A: I see. When will he return?
　　我知道了。他什麼時候回來？

B: He'll be back next Monday. 他下星期一會回來。

A： All right. I'll call again Monday.
　　好吧，我星期一再打。

B： May I have your name？
　　請問尊姓大名？

A： Paul Brown. 保羅‧布朗。

B： Mr. Paul Brown. 保羅‧布朗先生。

A： That's right. 是的。

B： I'll tell Mr. Lin you called when he returns.
　　林先生回來我會告訴他你打電話來。

A： Thank you. 謝謝你。

【註】

　　head〔hɛd〕n. 主管；首長
　　export〔'ɛksport〕n. 外銷；輸出
　　chief〔tʃif〕n. 主管；首長
　　go on a trip 去旅行
　　return〔rɪ'tɜn〕v. 回來

58. *Messenger Service. May I help you*?

傳信服務部。有什麼要效勞的嗎？

📞 **對話精華**

* Will you have Mr. David Lin call me *as soon as possible*?

  請你儘快要林大衛先生打電話給我好嗎？
* May I have *the number to be called*?

  請問你電話號碼？
* *I can be reached at* 545-7890.

  打 545-7890 可以找到我。

Dialogue

A: Hello. 喂。

B: Hello, operator. I'd like to speak to a friend of mine, but he doesn't have a telephone. Is there any way I can have him call me?

  喂，接線生，我要和我的一位朋友說話，不過他沒有電話。有沒有辦法叫他打電話給我？

A: Yes, I'll connect you with the Messenger Service. You give your friend's name and address to them, and they will give him your message.

  有的，我幫你聯絡傳信服務部，你把你朋友的名字和住址給他們，他們就會把你的消息傳給他。

C: Messenger Service. May I help you?

  傳信服務部。有什麼要效勞的嗎？

B： Yes, will you have Mr. David Lin call me as soon as possible？ He lives at 112, Park Road, Los Angeles, the United States.

是的，請你儘快要林大衛先生打電話給我好嗎？他住在美國洛杉磯公園路 112 號。

C： Yes. Mr. David Lin who lives at 112, Park Road, Los Angeles, the United States. May I have your name and the number to be called？

好的。美國洛杉磯公園路 112 號的林大衛先生。請問你大名和電話號碼？

B： Yes, my name is John, and I can be reached at 545-7890 between 2 and 5, and at 544-2468 after 6. By the way, what's the charge for this service？

好的。我的名字是約翰，兩點到五點之間打 545-7890 可以跟我聯絡，六點以後打 544-2468 可以找到我。對了，這項服務費用是多少？

C： It will be the total of a messenger charge and a toll charge.

總共要付傳信費用和長途電話費。

【註】

messenger service 傳信服務部

message〔'mɛsɪdʒ〕*n.* 信息；傳話

reach〔ritʃ〕*v.*（以電話）聯絡

total〔'totl〕*n.* 總額

toll〔tol〕*n.* 長途電話費

🕰 台灣與美加地區時刻對照表 🕰

台灣	西海岸時區	山岳時區	中部時區	東部時區
時差 時間	－ 16	－ 15	－ 14	－ 13
0	8 A.M.	9 A.M.	10 A.M.	11 A.M.
1	9	10	11	12
2	10	11	12	13
3	11	12	13	14
4	12	13	14	15
5	13	14	15	16
6	14	15	16	17
7	15	16	17	18
8	16	17	18	19
9	17	18	19	20
10	18	19	20	21
11	19	20	21	22
12	20	21	22	23
13	21	22	23	0
14	22	23	0	1
15	23	0	1	2
16	0	1	2	3
17	1	2	3	4
18	2	3	4	5
19	3	4	5	6
20	4	5	6	7
21	5	6	7	8
22	6	7	8	9
23	7	8	9	10

★ 註：阿拉斯加與夏威夷不在美國本土上，與台灣的時差為 –18 小時。

第 **3** 章 國際電話必備常識

" What You Need
 to Know for
International Calls "

國 際 電 話

　　隨著交通工具的發達，出國旅行已非常普遍，因此，打國際電話的機會也很多。當然也就應該具備必要的常識和語言能力，以下介紹一些重要的常識：

一、國際電話的種類

1. **Station Call**（叫號電話）：Station-to-Station Call
   這是指定對方電話號碼的國際電話，和國內的長途電話相同，對方接聽後開始計費。目前國內可以直接撥號的國家很多，可查閱電話號碼簿或詢問電信局。

2. **Personal Call**（叫人電話）：Person-to-Person Call
   這是指定對方姓名的國際電話，要加算指名費用，但是如果被指名的人不在時，則不計費。

3. **Collect Call**（對方付費電話）
   這是由對方付費的電話，由接線生幫忙問對方是否願意付費，費用和指名電話的費用相同。

4. **Credit Card Call**（利用信用卡記帳的電話）
   先向電信局申請信用卡，再帶此卡出國，打國際電話時使用，電話費由信用卡契約中所指定的公司或個人支付。

　　國際電話有上面這四個種類，可以依照時間和場合的不同來運用。如果想知道家裏是否平安無事，就打叫號電話；特別想和某個人說話時，打叫人電話；想節省旅費，打對方付費的電話。此外，常常需要打國際電話的人，則可以利用信用卡打電話。

其他還有**會議電話**（ conference call ）。會議電話是指對方同時接兩支以上的電話，好像在開會似的用電話談話。不過此種電話不能用叫號電話的方式打，而且要附加特別費用。

另外也有**船舶電話**，是在外國的船舶上，經由海岸電信局打出的電話，或在本國的船舶上，經由海岸電信局打出的電話。這種船舶電話是專門的電話，使用機會很少。

二、打國際電話的方法

在外國的旅館要打電話時，可以向旅館的櫃台、總機申請；如果在朋友的家裏或公司打電話，要先告訴接線生，請她在通話完畢後，告知電話費用。

打國際電話時必須注意的事項有下列十項：

1. 說出電話的種類：叫號電話、指名電話…等。通話結束後不可以更改電話的種類。
2. 說出對方的國名、地名：台灣台北（ Taipei, Taiwan ）或法國巴黎（ Paris, France ）。
3. 說出對方的區域號碼（ area code ）、電話號碼（ telephone number ）。如台北的區域號碼是 02，電話號碼是 700-0787（ 七位數 ）。
4. 說出對方的姓名：明確地說出先生（ Mr. ）、太太（ Mrs. ）、或小姐（ Miss ）。叫號電話則不必說出此項。
5. 說出自己的姓名、電話號碼；如果是在旅館打電話，要說自己的房間號碼。
6. 注意時差：預先知道時差，以免打擾對方。
7. 姓名或住址的發音不清楚時，將英文字母拼給接線生聽。
8. 打錯地方或電話線有雜音、干擾時，要立刻切斷電話重打。
9. 不清楚對方的電話號碼時，則說出對方姓名和住址，請電信局調查。
10. 在旅館打電話，通常要付手續費。

　　此外，不知道對方的電話號碼，但是知道對方所住的旅館名稱和地名時，還是可以打國際電話和對方聯絡上。另一方面，若是不確定對方是否住在那裏，也可以問旅館的服務員，因爲旅館都有住宿者的名册，可以查明。

　　另外，如果有由國外來的對方付費的電話，接線生會用英文直接說："*We have a collect call for you from Mr. Miles in London. Will you accept the charges*？"（這是由倫敦的邁爾斯先生打來的對方付費電話。你願意付費嗎？）如果願意，就說 "*Yes, I will.*" 但是聽不懂接線生說的話時，不能隨便說：「Yes.」（好。）要說："*Taipei operator, please*！"（請找台北接線生！），請台北接線生幫忙翻譯。

三、緊急電話的使用方法

　　美國有**緊急電話**（ emergency call ）的服務項目，即因爲緊急的事情，請接線生中斷通話中的電話。打緊急電話時，要先撥一個" 0 "，再將請求的事情向接線生說明。例如：

I've been calling 700-0787 for over one hour, but the line is still busy. Would you interrupt the conversation, please？（ *It's an emergency.* ）

我打 700-0787 打了一個小時了，但是電話仍然佔線，請你切斷好嗎？（這是緊急事件。）

這時接線生會問對方是否要接這通電話（ Would you accept an emergency call？）對方同意後，接線生會問打緊急電話者的姓名，和他想通話者的姓名，然後向對方說：

Excuse me. This is the operator. You have an emergency call from ~ to…. Hang up for a minute, please.

（對不起！有~打給…的緊急電話。請將電話掛斷一會兒。）

打緊急電話的人，在申請打緊急電話後，要掛斷電話等兩、三分鐘，再打給對方。緊急電話雖然方便，但有時會給人添麻煩，最好儘量不要打。

四、使用外國電話號碼簿的方法

看電話簿查電話號碼，雖然比直接打電話問電信局查號台要麻煩，但是應該要知道使用電話簿的方法，善用利用，節省電話費的開支。

不論哪個國家，都有兩種電話簿，即職業類的電話簿和姓名類的電話簿。前者在英國、美國、加拿大，稱為 *yellow pages*，因為電話簿是用黃顏色的紙印成的;後著稱為 *white pages*，因為是用白顏色的紙印成的。澳洲的職業類電信簿是粉紅色的，稱為 *classified jobs section*。不同的顏色很容易使人區分出電話簿的種類。

使用電話簿的方法，和國內的幾乎相同;不過外國是依照英文字母的順序排列，先將姓氏排在前面，後面有逗點，再排名字。人名和字典或百科全書的排法一樣，如果是John H. Smith則排成 *Smith, John H.* 地址通常能用縮寫，請參考下面列舉的美國各州及主要都市名的縮寫表。

❖ 美 國 各 州 ❖

Alabama	- Ala.	Minnesota	- Minn.
Alaska	- Alas.	Mississippi	- Miss.
Arizona	- Ariz.	Missouri	- Mo.
Arkansas	- Ark.	Montana	- Mont.
California	- Cal	Nebraska	- Nebr.
Colorado	- Colo.	Nevada	- Ne.
Connecticut	- Conn.	New Hampshire	- N. H.
Delaware	- Del.	New Jersey	- N. J.

Florida	- Fla.	New Mexico	- N. Mex. (M.)
Georgia	- Ga.	New York	- N. Y.
Hawaii	- Hawaii	North Carolina	- N. C.
Idaho	- Ida.	North Dakota	- N. Dak
Illinois	- Ill.	Ohio	- Ohio
Indiana	- Ind.	Oklahoma	- Okla.
Iowa	- Iowa	Oregon	- Oreg
Kansas	- Kans.	Pennsylvania	- Pa.
Kentucky	- Ky.	Rhode Island	- R. I.
Louisiana	- La.	South Carolina	- S. C.
Maine	- Maine	South Dakota	- S. Dak
Maryland	- Md.	Tennessee	- Tenn.
Massachusetts	- Mass.	Texas	- Tex.
Michigan	- Mich.	Utah	- Utah
Vermont	- Vt.	West Virginia	- W. Va.
Virginia	- Va.	Wisconsin	- Wis.
Washington	- Wash.	Wyoming	- Wyo.

❖ 美 國 主 要 都 市 ❖

Las Vegas	- L. V.	Los Angeles	- L. A.
New Orleans	- N. O.	New York	- N. Y.
San Francisco	- S. F.	Washington D. C.	- D. C.

查職業類電話簿時，先看目錄查職業，再看公司或店名。例如想查 *Peter Ford* 糖果糕餅店，就先看目錄，查糖果糕餅業（ confectionery ），然後再查 PETER FORD CONFECTIONERY。電話簿內一定有區域號碼，另外，甚至也有費用表、時差表、巴士時刻表和交通道路地圖，是可以常利用的工具書。

五、在國外使用公用電話的方法：

在國外打公用電話，首先必須曉得一些基本常識，才能達到方便聯絡的效果。美國市區的電話，全是直撥電話（a direct call），只要投入10分硬幣，再撥號碼盤就可以了。如果區域不同，則先撥區域號碼（area code），再撥電話號碼。不爲同一區域，不能用10分打電話的場合，接線生會叫你先付頭三分鐘的費用（***Deposit fifty cents, please.*** 請付50分。）在小鄉鎮使用公共電話，如果希望對方付費（collect call），就請接線生處理。這時先撥「0」，告訴接線生想通話的市名，例如想從鄉下打到洛杉磯的話，就說：***I'd like***（＝want）***to call Los Angeles.*** 當接線生和洛杉磯地區的接線生取得聯絡後，你再告話訴他對方的電話號碼和市名。這時接線生也會問你所用的公用電話號碼（***What's your number, please*** ？）回答用 ***My number is*** ～. 然後再照接線生的指示，投入應投的費用。接線生會接著說：***Hold on, please.***（請稍候。）你就拿著電話聽筒等對方的回應。如果當地的電話線被佔用了，接線生會說：***Hang up a moment, please.***（請掛斷電話一會兒。）當對方的電話接通後，接線生會再打電話通知你。

要對方付費的時候，等當地的接線生說話時，務必要說 ***I want to place a collect call to Los Angeles.*** 或 ***A collect call, please.*** 然後接線生會問你：***May I have the name of the party*** 〔***person***〕***who***（**m**）***you want to talk to*** ？（請告訴我你想通話的人的姓名好嗎？）這時你要清楚地說：***I want to talk to Mr. Liang. L-I-A-N-G***（我想和梁先生說話。）因爲外國人對中國人的姓氏（last name）不熟悉，所以最好慢慢拼音給接線生聽。注意當你要開始和對方講話之前，也就是你剛和接線生結束對話時，當初你投入的10分硬幣會掉入退幣口，不要忘了取回。

六、其他常用的句子

1. 問電話費用

I want to place a call to Japan. Will you tell me the charges?

我要打越洋電話到日本，請告訴我費用好嗎？

2. 問等候的時間

I want to place a call to England. How long will it take?

我要打電話到英國，請問要等多久？

3. 問當地的時間

I want to place a call to Tokyo. What time is it now over there?

我想打長途電話到東京，請問那兒現在幾點？

What is the time in Hong Kong at 9 p.m. here in Washington?

華盛頓下午九點相當於香港幾點鐘？

4. 預約打電話的時間

I want to place a call to Copenhagen at noon our time.

我將在此地正午時間〔12:00〕打電話到哥本哈根。

5. 請求再接上通話中途切斷的電話

I was cut off. Will you connect me again?

我的電話被切斷了，請再幫我接通好嗎？

6. 接線生接錯電話時

I've been connected to the wrong party (a wrong number).

我的電話接錯了。

7. 電話無法打通的情況

A. 電話線正被佔線

Operator : The lines to Madrid are busy now. Will
you hold the line, please ?
　　　　到馬德里的線路正講話中，請您稍等。

Lin : Certainly. 好的。

B. 對方在通話中

Operator : Boston 785-6236 is busy now. Will you
hold the line, please ?
　　　　波士頓 785-6236 在講話中，請稍候。

Lin : All right. 好。

Then will you try another number, 785-6339 ?
　　那麼，請幫我接另一個號碼 —— 785-6339 好嗎 ?

Will you try again in one hour ?
　　請在一小時後再幫我接一次好嗎 ?

I have to go out now. Will you call me back
at ten o'clock tonight ?
　　我現在必須出門，今晚十點再打給我好嗎 ?

C. 對方沒有人接電話

Operator : Manila 359-6006 doesn't answer.
　　　　馬尼拉 359-6006 沒人接。

Lin : Please cancel the call. 那麼，請取消這通電話。

D. 電話故障

Operator : I'm sorry, but the telephone is out of order.
　　　　對不起，對方電話故障。

Lin : I see. Cancel the call, please.
　　　我知道了，請取消這通電話。

E. 電話號碼錯誤

Operator : Detroit 594-5188 is the wrong number.
　　　　　Will you check it again?
　　　　　底特律 594-5188 這個號碼是錯誤的。你要不
　　　　　要再檢查一遍？

Lin : I see. Cancel the call, please. Oh, I'm sorry I
　　　gave you the wrong number. The correct number
　　　is 463-8231.
　　　我知道了。請等一下。喔，我給錯號碼了，正確的號碼應
　　　該是 463-8231。

第 **4** 章 國際電話實況會話

" Conversation for
    International Calls "

59. *How about the charge*?
費用呢？

📞 **對話精華**

* Will you *quote the charges*?
  你們通知費用嗎？
* Don't you have *special discount rates*?
  你們有沒有特別的折扣？
* *The details are given* on the back of the telephone directory. 詳情在電話簿後面有。

Dialogue

A： Hello. 喂。

B： Hello. Overseas operator. May I help you, sir?
　　　喂，國際電話台。有什麼可效勞的嗎？先生。

A： Yes, I'm going to call Taiwan some time next week, and I'd like to find out the time difference and the charges.
　　　是的，我下星期某個時間要打電話到台灣去。我想查查時差和費用。

B： The time difference between Los Angeles and Taiwan is 16 hours. For example, if you place a call at 10 p.m. Monday here, it will be 2 p.m. on Tuesday in Taiwan.
　　　洛杉磯和台灣的時差是十六個小時。譬如說，如果你在這裏星期一晚上十點打電話，台灣就是星期二下午兩點。

A : I see. How about the charges ? 我懂了。費用呢？

B : The charges vary according to the type of call you make. The cheapest is a station-to-station call, then a person-to-person call. The minimum charge will apply for the first three minutes, then each additional minute will be charged.

費用根據你打的電話種類而不同。最便宜的是叫號電話，然後是叫人電話。前三分鐘是最起碼的基本費，後來多加的每分鐘都要另外算。

A : Will you quote the charges ? 你們會告訴我費用嗎？

B : Yes, if you notify the operator when you place your call. 會的，只要你在打電話時通知一下接線生。

A : Don't you have special discount rates such as night rates and Sunday rates ? 你們晚上和星期天有沒有特別的折扣？

B : Yes, we do. The details are given on the back of the telephone directory, so will you please read it ? 有的。詳情在電話簿後面有，請你看看好嗎？

A : OK, I will. Thank you for your information. 好，我會的。謝謝你告訴我。

B : You're welcome. Good-bye. 不客氣。再見。

【註】

> *find out* 查知　　*time difference* 時差
> charge〔tʃɑrdʒ〕*n.* 費用　　vary〔'vɛrɪ〕*v.* 不同；改變
> discount〔'dɪskaʊnt〕*n.* 折扣　　*apply for* 適用於
> minimum〔'mɪnəməm〕*n.* 最小量
> additional〔ə'dɪʃən!〕*adj.* 附加的；額外的
> notify〔'notə,faɪ〕*v.* 通知

60. *Is this a station-to-station call*?
是叫號電話嗎？

☎ **對話精華**

* Is this the *overseas operator*? 是國際電話台嗎？
* I want to *place an overseas call*.
  我要打一通越洋電話。
* *Where are you calling*? 你要打到哪裏？
* *I'm calling Taiwan.* 我要打到台灣。
* Is this *a station-to-station call*? 是叫號電話嗎？
* Could you *tell me the time and charges* after this
  call? 通話後請告訴我時間和費用好嗎？

Dialogue

A : Is this the overseas operator? 是國際電話台嗎？

B : Yes, it is. May I help you? 是的，要我爲您效勞嗎？

A : I want to place an overseas call.
    我要打一通越洋電話。

B : Where are you calling? 你要打到哪裏？

A : I'm calling Taiwan. 我要打到台灣。

B : What city in Taiwan are you calling?
    打到台灣什麼城市？

A : I want to call Taipei. 打到台北。

B : May I have the number in Taipei?
    請告訴我台北的號碼好嗎？

A : Of course. The telephone number is（02）700-0787.
當然。電話號碼是（02）700-0787。

B : The telephone number is 02-700-0787.
號碼是 02-700-0787。

A : That's right. 對的。

B : May I have your telephone number ?
請告訴我你的電話號碼好嗎 ?

A : Los Angeles 737-5595. 洛杉磯 737-5595。

B : Los Angeles 7-3-7-5-5-9-5. 洛杉磯 7-3-7-5-5-9-5。

A : Right. 對。

B : Is this a station-to-station call ? 是叫號電話嗎 ?

A : Yes, it is. Could you tell me the time and charges
after this call ?
是的。通話後請告訴我時間和費用好嗎 ?

B : Certainly, sir. I'll call you back after the call. Will you
hold the line, please ?
當然，先生。通話完畢後我會打給你。請稍候好嗎 ?

A : All right, thank you. 好的，謝謝你。

【註】

station-to-station call 叫號電話（指定某一個電話號碼而撥的國際電話，
不指定某人接，只要有人接到，通話之後便須付電話費。）

overseas〔'ovɚ'siz〕*adj.* 國外的；越洋的

place〔ples〕*v.* 撥（電話）

charge〔tʃɑrdʒ〕*n.* 費用

61. *Operator, do I have to wait a long time*?

接線生，我需要等很久嗎？

📞 **對話精華**

* I'd like *to place an overseas call* to Taipei, Taiwan.
  我要打通越洋電話到台灣台北。
* Do I have to wait a long time?
  我需要等很久嗎？
* I think I can *get your call through* in a minute.
  我想我可以馬上幫你接通。

Dialogue

A : Overseas operator. May I help you?
國際電話台。有什麼可以效勞的嗎？

B : I'd like to place an overseas call to Taipei, Taiwan.
我要打通越洋電話到台灣台北。

A : May I have the telephone number in Taipei, please?
請你給我台北的電話號碼好嗎？

B : Yes, the number is 02-700-0787.
好。號碼是 02-700-0787。

A : That's 02-700-0787. 02-700-0787。

B : That's right. 對。

A： May I have your number, please?
　　請問你的電話號碼?

B： Yes, it's 355-300. 好。355-300。

A： Thank you. Will you hold the line, please?
　　謝謝你。請稍候好嗎?

B： Operator, do I have to wait a long time?
　　接線生，我需要等很久嗎?

A： No, I think I can get your call through in a minute.
　　不，我想我可以馬上幫你接通。

【註】

　get through （電話）接通

62. *This is a person-to-person call.*
我打叫人電話。

☎ **對話精華**

* Will you please *spell out* that name？
  請你拼出那名字好嗎？

* Will you *hang up*？ 請掛斷電話好嗎？

* I'll call you back *as soon as the connection is made*.
  一接通我就馬上跟你聯絡。

Dialogue

A : Overseas operator. May I help you？
  國際電話台。有什麼可以效勞的嗎？

B : Yes. I want to call Taipei, Taiwan. This is a person-to-person call.
  是的。我要打到台灣台北。我打叫人電話。

A : All right, sir. May I have the number in Taipei, please？
  好的，先生。請給我台北的號碼好嗎？

B : The number in Taipei is 02-700-0787.
  台北電話是 02-700-0787。

A : That's Taipei 02-700-0787. Who would you like to speak to, sir？
  台北 02-700-0787。你找誰聽電話，先生？

B : I'd like to speak with Miss Jenny Huang.
  我找黃珍妮小姐聽電話。

A : Will you please spell out that name？
　　請你拼出那名字好嗎？

B : Yes, it's J-e-n-n-y, and the last name is H-u-a-n-g.
　　好，J-e-n-n-y，姓是 H-u-a-n-g。

A : Thank you. That's Miss Jenny Huang. May I have your name and number, please？
　　謝謝你。是黃珍妮小姐。請告訴我你的名字和號碼好嗎？

B : My name is David Lin, and I'm calling from 212-545-3721.
　　我叫林大衛。我的號碼是 212-545-3721。

A : Mr. David Lin, and the number is 212-545-3721.
　　林大衛先生。號碼是 212-545-3721。

B : That's correct. 對。

A : Will you hang up and wait for a minute？ I'll call you back as soon as the connection is made.
　　請掛斷等一會兒好嗎？一接通我就馬上跟你聯絡。

(*three minutes later*)（三分鐘後）

A : Hello. Is this Mr. Lin？ 喂，林先生嗎？

B : Yes, speaking. 是的，我就是。

A : This is the overseas operator. Your party in Taipei is on now. Please go ahead, sir.
　　這裏是國際電話台，台北那邊來接了。請講話，先生。

B : Thank you. 謝謝你。

【註】

spell out 拼出來　　*hang up* 掛斷電話
connection〔kə'nɛkʃən〕*n.* 連接

63. *I want to place a long distance collect call to Taiwan.*

我要打通對方付費的長途電話到台灣。

📞 **對話精華**

* I want to *place a long distance collect call* to Taiwan.
  我要打通對方付費的長途電話到台灣。
* Who would you like to talk to？ 你想找誰聽電話？
* We'll call you back. *Will you hang up and wait, please*？ 我們會打給你。請掛斷稍等好嗎？

Dialogue

A： This is the overseas operator. 國際電話台。

B： I want to place a long distance collect call to Taiwan.
   我要打通對方付費的長途電話到台灣。

A： What city are you calling？ 你要打到哪個城市？

B： I'm calling Taipei, and the number is（02）707-1413。
   台北。電話是（02）707-1413。

A： Taipei（02）707-1413？ 台北（02）707-1413？

B： Yes. 對。

A： May I have your name and telephone number？
   請問尊姓大名和電話號碼？

B： This is Mr. Joseph Lee 479-8468. 我是 479-8468 李約瑟。

A： Mr. Lee. Who would you like to talk to？
   李先生。你想找誰聽電話？

B： I'd like to talk to Mr. or Mrs. Lin. 林先生或林太太。

A： All right. We'll call you back. Will you hang up and wait, please？ 好的。我們會打給你。請掛斷稍等好嗎？

B： Thank you. 謝謝你。

(a few seconds later)（片刻之後）

B： Hello. 喂。

A： This is the overseas telephone operator. Is this New York 479-8468？ 這裏是國際電話台。是紐約 479-8468 嗎？

B： Yes, it is. This is Mr. Lee speaking. 是的。我是李先生。

A： Will you hold the line, please？ 請不要掛斷好嗎？

(a few seconds later)（片刻之後）

A： Thank you for waiting. Mr. Lin in Taipei is on the line. Go ahead, please. 謝謝你等候。台北林先生來接了，請講話。

〔*C*〕 活用練習

1. Mr. Lin in Taipei is on the line. Go ahead, please.
   台北林先生來接了，請講話。
2. Your party is on the line, go ahead, please.
   對方接了，請講話。
3. On the line, go ahead. 來接了，請講話。
4. He is on the line, go ahead. 他來接了，請講話。
5. You are connected, go ahead, please.
   你們的線路接通了，請講話。

【註】

　　collect call 對方付費電話　　*on the line* 來接電話；在電話線上

64. *Who would you like to talk to, sir*?
你要找誰聽電話？先生。

📞 **對話精華**

* I'd like to *place a collect call* to Taipei, Taiwan.
  我要打通對方付費電話到台灣台北。

* Who would you like to talk to, sir?
  你要找誰聽電話？先生。

* Will you *hold on a minute*? 請你稍候好嗎？

Dialogue

A : Overseas operator. May I help you?
    國際電話台。有什麼可以效勞的嗎？

B : Hello, operator. I'd like to place a collect call to Taipei, Taiwan.
    喂，接線生，我要打通對方付費電話到台灣台北。

A : A collect call to Taiwan, sir?
    對方付費電話到台灣嗎？先生。

B : Yes, please. The number in Taipei is 02-700-0787.
    是的。台北的號碼是 02-700-0787。

A : The number is 02-700-0787. 號碼是 02-700-0787。

B : That's right. 對。

A : Who would you like to talk to, sir?
    你要找誰聽電話？先生。

B : I'd like to talk to Mrs. Lisa Brown.
    我找莎莉・布朗太太聽電話。

A : May I have your name and telephone number, please ?
　　請告訴我你的名字和電話號碼好嗎？

B : Yes, I'm Mr. Brown calling from Room 913, at Howard Johnson's Motor Lodge.
　　好，我是布朗先生，從霍華德‧詹森的汽車旅館 913 室打的電話。

A : Which Howard Johnson's, sir ?
　　哪個霍華德‧詹森的旅館？先生。

B : The number is 317-2711.
　　號碼是 317-2711 。

A : Will you hold on a minute, Mr. Brown ?
　　請你稍候好嗎？布朗先生。

【註】

motor〔'motɚ〕*n.* 汽車
lodge〔lɑdʒ〕*n.* 旅館

65. I'd like to make a credit card call to Taipei, Taiwan.

我要打通記帳電話到台灣台北。

☏ 對話精華

* I'd like to **make a credit card call to** Taipei, Taiwan.
  我要打通記帳電話到台灣台北。
* **Make it a station-to-station call,** please.
  我打叫號電話。
* We will **call you back** in 30 minutes.
  我們三十分鐘後會回電話給你。
* Sorry, I can't wait. **Please cancel it.**
  對不起，我不能等，請取消。

Dialogue

A : This is the overseas operator. 國際電話台。

B : I'd like to make a credit card call to Taipei, Taiwan.
   我要打通記帳電話到台灣台北。

A : Will you give me the credit card number ?
   請告訴我信用卡號碼好嗎？

B : Yes, 15F 670. 好的。15F 670。

A : 15F 670. 15F 670。

B : Right. 對。

A : What number are you calling? 你打幾號？

B : Taipei (02) 331-4060. 台北 (02) 331-4060。

A : 0-2-3-3-1-4-0-6-0？ Who would you like to talk to？
0-2-3-3-1-4-0-6-0 嗎？找誰聽電話？

B : Make it a station-to-station call, please.
我打叫號電話。

A : All right. May I have your number？
好的。請問你的號碼？

B : This is Chicago 339-5735.
芝加哥 339-5735。

A : Thank you. We'll call you back in 30 minutes. Will you hang up and wait, please？
謝謝你。我們三十分鐘後會回電話給你。請掛斷稍等好嗎？

B : 30 minutes？ 三十分鐘？

A : Yes. 是的。

B : Sorry, I can't wait. Please cancel it.
對不起，我不能等，請取消。

【註】

credit card 信用卡

cancel〔ˈkænsl̩〕*v.* 取消

66. *Charge, please.*

費用記帳。

📞 **對話精華**

* *By the way*, charge, please.
  順便一提，費用請記帳。
* May I have your credit card number, please ?
  請告訴我你的信用卡號碼好嗎？
* *Please make it a station call*.
  我打叫號電話。

Dialogue

A : Long distance operator. May I help you ?
  長途電話台。有什麼可以效勞的嗎？

B : Can I place an overseas call through you ?
  我能透過你打越洋電話嗎？

A : Yes, you can. Where are you calling, sir ?
  是的，可以。你要打到哪裏？先生。

B : I'd like to call Taipei, Taiwan. By the way, charge, please.
  我要打到台灣台北。順便一提，費用記帳。

A : May I have your credit card number, please ?
  請告訴我你的信用卡號碼好嗎？

B : Yes, my card number is 12K 345678.
  好的，我信用卡的號碼是 12K 345678。

A： 12K 345678？ 12K 345678？
B： Right. 對的。

A： May I have the number in Taipei, please？
　　請告訴我台北的號碼好嗎？
B： Yes, the number is 02-707-1413.
　　好的，號碼是 02-707-1413。

A： 02-707-1413？ 02-707-1413？
B： Yes, that's right. And please make it a station call.
　　是的。我打叫號電話。

A： All right, sir. May I have your number？
　　好的，先生。請告訴我你的號碼好嗎？
B： LA 8-4321. LA 8-4321。

A： Thank you. Will you please hang up and wait？ I'll call
　　you back in about 10 minutes.
　　謝謝你。請你掛斷等一會兒好嗎？我大概十分鐘後打給你。

【註】
　　through〔θru〕*prep.* 透過
　　Los Angeles〔lɔs'æŋgdʒələs〕*n.* 洛杉磯（簡稱 LA，為 California 州的
　　海港，美國第三大都市。）

67. A person-to-person call.
叫人電話。

📞 **對話精華**

* *I'd like to call Taipei, Taiwan.*
  我要打電話到台灣台北。
* Will you *pay for the call*?
  你付電話費嗎？
* Is this a *station-to-station call*? 是叫號電話嗎？
  No, *a person-to-person call*. 不是，是叫人電話。

Dialogue

A: This is the operator. 總機。

B: I'd like to call Taipei, Taiwan.
   我要打電話到台灣台北。

A: Will you pay for the call?
   你付電話費嗎？

B: Yes, I will. 是的，我付。

A: Thank you. What number are you calling?
   謝謝你。你打幾號？

B: Taipei 02-704-5525. 台北 02-704-5525。

A: Is this a station-to-station call?
   是叫號電話嗎？

B: No, a person-to-person call for Mr. Chou.
   不是，是叫人電話，找周先生。

A : Your name and room number, please.
　　請問你尊姓大名和房間號碼。

B : This is Mr. David Lin in room 543.
　　我是 543 室林大衛。

A : Mr. Lin in room 543 and Mr. Chou in Taipei 02-704-
　　5525 ? I'll place the call for you. Will you hang up and
　　wait, please ?
　　543 室林先生，台北 (02) 704-5525 的周先生。我會打電話給你。請
　　掛斷稍候好嗎？

B : Thank you. 謝謝你。

A : You are welcome. 不客氣。

【註】

　pay for　付～的費用

68. I'd like to place an overseas call to Taipei, Taiwan.

我要打通越洋電話到台灣台北。

☎ **對話精華**

* I'd like to *place an overseas call* to Taipei, Taiwan.
  我要打通越洋電話到台灣台北。
* Will you pay for the call? 你付電話費嗎?
  No, I want to *reverse the charges*. 不,由對方付。
* I'll *connect you with* the overseas telephone operator.
  我替你接國際電話台。
* I'll *ring the number for you*. 我替你撥號。

Dialogue

A : This is the operator. 總機。

B : I'd like to place an overseas call to Taipei, Taiwan.
    我要打通越洋電話到台灣台北。

A : To Taipei, Taiwan? Will you pay for the call?
    到台灣台北?你付電話費嗎?

B : No, I want to reverse the charges.
    不,由對方付。

A : Is this a collect call?
    是對方付費電話嗎?

B : Yes, it is. 是的。

A : Then, I'll connect you with the overseas telephone operator. Will you please place the call with her?
那麼我給你接國際電話台。請你打給她好嗎?

B : All right. 好的。

A : One moment, please. I'll ring the number for you.
請稍候。我替你撥號。

🎧 活用練習

1. I'd like to place an overseas call. 我要打通越洋電話。

2. I want to make an overseas call.

3. I want to place an overseas call.

【註】

reverse〔rɪ'vɝs〕v. 轉換;調換
ring〔rɪŋ〕v. 撥(電話)

69. *My party has cancelled the call now.*

我這邊的通話人現在已經取消這通電話了。

📞 **對話精華**

* He is out *right now*. 他現在不在。
* My party *has cancelled the call* now.
  我這邊的通話人現在已經取消這通電話了。

Dialogue

A: This is Taipei, Taiwan. May I speak to Mr. Haber Chen of the Sales Department?
這裏是台灣台北。請門市部的陳哈勃先生聽電話好嗎?

B: I'm sorry, he is out right now. 對不起,他現在不在。

A: Do you know when he'll be back?
你知道他什麼時候回來嗎?

B: He will be back sometime this afternoon. But I'm sorry, I can't tell you exactly what time.
他下午會回來。不過抱歉,我無法告訴你確實時間。

A: I see. 知道了。

B: May I take a message? 要不要留個話?

A: One moment, please. (*a few seconds late*) My party has cancelled the call now. Thank you.
請稍候。(片刻之後) 我這邊的通話人現在已經取消這通電話了。
謝謝你。

B: You're welcome. 不客氣。

70. *Operator, my party doesn't understand English.*

接線生，對方不懂英文。

☎ **對話精華**

* My party doesn't understand English.
  對方不懂英文。
* I will *ask for a language assistance is Taipei*.
  我請台北的語言助理。
* Please don't worry. 請別擔心。
* Thank you very much. 非常謝謝你。

Dialogue

A : Operator, my party doesn't understand English. Since
  this is a collect call, I hope she will accept it.
  接線生，對方不懂英文。因為這是對方付費電話，我希望她會接受。

B : Just a minute, Mr. Lin. I will ask for a language assistance in Taipei. Please don't worry.
  請稍等，林先生。我請台北的語言助理。請別擔心。

A : Oh, thank you very much. 哦，非常謝謝你。

B : You're welcome. Just hold the line, please.
  不客氣。請稍候。

【註】

accept〔 ək'sɛpt 〕*v.* 接受　　***ask for*** 請求
assistance〔 ə'sɪstəns 〕*n.* 助理；援助　　worry〔'wɝɪ〕*v.* 擔心

71. *Your party's line is busy.*
對方在講話中。

📞 **對話精華**

* All right, sir. 好的，先生。
* Hello, ***your party's line is busy***. 喂，對方在講話中
* ***Never mind***. 沒關係。
* You're welcome. 不客氣。

Dialogue

A : Long Distance. May I help you ?
　　長途電話台。有什麼可以效勞的嗎？

B : Yes, I'd like to place an overseas call to Taipei,
　　Taiwan. 是的，我要打通越洋電話到台灣台北。

A : All right, sir. Is this a station call or a personal call ?
　　好的，先生。是叫號還是叫人？

B : A station call, please. The number is 02-700-0787.
　　叫號。電話是 02-700-0787。

A : May I have your number, please ?
　　請告訴我你的號碼好嗎？

B : My number is 123-4566.
　　我的號碼是 123-4566。

A : Will you please hold the line ?
　　請稍候好嗎？

(*after a moment*) (片刻之後)

Hello, your party's line is busy. Would you care to wait, sir ?
喂，對方在講話中。你要不要等一下？先生。

B : No, never mind, then. I'll try again in about two hours. Thank you, operator.
不，那麼沒關係。我大概兩個小時後再試試看。謝謝你，接線生。

A : You're welcome. Thank you for calling.
不客氣。謝謝你的電話。

【註】

　　The line is busy. （電話）講話中。
　　Never mind. 沒關係。

72. *Could you call him back tomorrow morning*？

你明天早上再打來好嗎？

☎ 對話精華

* We *have a call* for Mr. Ike Park.
  我們有通艾克・派克先生的電話。
* Could you *call him back* tomorrow morning？
  你明天早上再打來好嗎？

Dialogue

A： This is the overseas operator in Taipei, Taiwan. We have a call for Mr. Ike Park.
這裏是台灣台北的國際電話台。我們有通艾克・派克先生的電話。

B： I'm sorry, he has gone home already.
對不起，他已經回家了。

A： Oh, is that right？ Do you have his home number？
哦，是嗎？你有他家的電話號碼嗎？

B： I'm sorry, we don't. Could you call him back tomorrow morning？ He'll come to his office at nice o'clock.
抱歉，我們沒有。你明天早上再打來好嗎？他九點會到辦公室。

A： All right. 好的。

B： Thank you. 謝謝你。

【註】

call〔kɔl〕*n.* 電話

73. *When he comes in, I'll tell him he had a call.*

他進來時，我會告訴他有電話。

對話精華

* Can you tell me *what time he'll be in*?
  你能不能夠告訴我他什麼時候會在？
* When he comes in, I'll tell him *he had a call*.
  他來時我會告訴他有電話。

Dialogue

A: May I speak to Mr. Ike Park?
請艾克·派克先生聽電話好嗎？

B: I'm sorry, he hasn't come in yet.
對不起，他還沒來。

A: Can you tell me what time he'll be in?
你能告訴我他什麼時候會在嗎？

B: Within half an hour, I think.
我想再過半小時吧。

A: I'll call him back in about thirty minutes then.
那麼我大概再過三十分鐘再打給他。

B: Thank you, operator. When he comes in, I'll tell him he had a call.
謝謝你，接線生。他來時我會告訴他有電話。

A: Thank you, sir. 謝謝你，先生。

B: You're welcome. 不客氣。

74. *What was the number I gave you*?
我給你幾號？

📞 **對話精華**

* ***There is no David Lin at that number***.
  那號碼沒有林大衛這個人。
* Will you *check the number again*?
  你要不要再查對一下號碼？
* Let me try again. 我再試試。

Dialogue

A： Operator, I'd like to make a person-to-person call to Taipei, Taiwan. The number is 02-700-0789, and I want to speak to Mr. David Lin.

接線生，我要打通叫人電話到台灣台北。號碼是 02-700-0787。我找林大衛先生聽電話。

B： To Mr. David Lin, at 02-700-0787？

找 02-700-0789 的林大衛先生？

A： Yes, that's right. 是的，沒錯。

B： May I have your name and telephone number？

請問你的名字和電話號碼？

A： My name is John Brown, and the phone number is 390-8001.

我的名字叫約翰・布朗，電話號碼是 390-8001。

B： Mr. Brown, will you hold the line, please？

布朗先生，請稍候好嗎？

(*after a while*) (片刻之後)

Mr. Brown, there is no David Lin at that number.
Will you check the number again?
布朗先生，那號碼沒有林大衛這個人。你要不要再查對一下號碼？

A : What was the number I gave you, operator?
我給你幾號？接線生。

B : It's 02-700-0789. 02-700-0789。

A : Oh, I'm sorry. It should have been 0787, not 0789.
哦，對不起。應該是 0787，不是 0789。

B : OK. Let me try again.
好，我再試試。

【註】

check〔tʃɛk〕*v.* 查對

75. *This is the overseas operator in Taipei.*
We have a call for Mr. Lin.

這是台北國際電話台。
有通林先生的電話。

☎ **對話精華**

* We have a collect call for you from Mr. Huang. Will you *accept the charges* ?
  有通黃先生打給你的對方付費的電話，你接受嗎？

Dialogue

A : This is the Overseas Operator in Taipei. We have a call for Mr. Lin.
   這裏是台北國際電話台。有通林先生的電話。

B : This is he speaking. 我就是。

A : We have a collect call for you from Mr. Kang Huang in Taipei. Will you accept the charges, Mr. Lin ?
   有通黃先生打給你的對方付費的電話，你接受？林先生。

B : Yes, I will. 是的，我接受。

A : Thank you. Hold the line, please.
   謝謝你。請不要掛斷。

(*to Mr. Huang in Taipei*)（對台北黃先生說話）

Thank you for waiting. Mr. Lin in New York is on the line. Go ahead, please.
謝謝你等候。紐約的林先生來了。請講話。

You Can *CALL* Me

Call-in 說英語

拿起電話，馬上就可說英語！

結合電腦與通訊科技，欣語社為您設計「**克拉瑪空中外語交談園地**」，以最方便、經濟、效率的休閒式方法，使您學習外語會話成為舉手之勞。

1. 以會員制**購卡**方式，一卡可通美、日語。經您授權，別人亦可使用。

2. 在系統的時間內（全年無休），只要有電話機，可隨時地和老外練習外語，而不耽誤您正常作息。

3. 會員卡無使用期限，且每次談話**時間亦無限制**。

4. 電腦自動計時，並告知您剩餘時間。

5. 您的花費只有傳統一對一費用的一半或更少，同時省去餐費、交通費及時間。

6. 每次對談之前您可設定喜歡的話題，及預備些字彙或造句，我們的外籍會員依據您所表達之外語程度，以適當之談話速度，及深淺字句和您雙向溝通，讓您在閒談式的心情下，增進外語能力和信心。

7. 假設您正從事國際商務，只需一通電話，便有外籍秘書或活字典在電話彼端，即刻為您解決外文上的疑難。

8. 您每次談話對象，可能都是不同之外籍會員，除可加強適應不同之腔調外，亦可增加不同生活體驗及擴展國際視野。

★ **入會費及通話費如下：**

入會費	美語卡（日本語卡）		通話費
500 元	每次購	10 小時	2,800 元
		20 小時	5,200 元
		40 小時	10,000 元
免費	續卡之會員（本人）		

☞凡購買 *You Can Call Me* 一書的讀者，可利用書後所附之劃撥單、訂購單，享受**免入會費**的優待。

★ 通話時間

美語卡：早上 9 點至晚上 12 點　　**日本語卡：晚上 7 點至晚上 11 點。**
☞ 通話專線 *12 線，不用擔心佔線。*

★ 購卡方式：

1. 利用附表之**劃撥單**（帳號 18291332，戶名：欣語社）、**信用卡訂購
   單**，填妥即可。
2. 來社購卡，週一至週六 AM10:00 ～ PM10:00
3. 送卡收款：暫限台北市內，但須配合本社時間。

The Foreign Members（Teachers）Reference
外籍會員背景參考表

NAME	DEGREE	EDUCATION	NATIONALITY
Mr. Chris Smith	Bachelor	Yale, Maryland	USA
Mr. Tom	Bachelor	James Madison	USA
Mr. George	Bachelor	Rutgers University	USA
Mr. Steve	Bachelor	UCLA	USA
Mr. Mark	Bachelor	UCLA	USA
Mr. John	Bachelor	Hawaii University	USA
Ms. Diana	Master	U.C. Berkeley	USA
Mr. Gregor	Bachelor	U.C. Santa Cruz	USA
Ms. Marie	Master	Irvine MBA	A.B.C
Mr. Romeo	Bachelor	Mapua Institution	OS Chinese
Ms. Brenda	Bachelor	Philippine University	Filipino
Ms. Jeanette	Bachelor	Delasaile University	OS Chinese
Ms. Emily	Bachelor	Delasaile University	OS Chinese

凡參加「克拉瑪空中外語交談園地」之會員，除免費提供 TOPICS 資料，
讓您加強聽講會話能力，我們亦增加下列服務項目：

★ 英文書信、商業文件、寫作等之修改與修辭　☎ *(02) 2751-6278*

已加入（克拉瑪空中外語交談園地）之會員才有附帶服務，讓您除

加強外語會話能力外，亦可提升層次，說寫俱佳。其計費方式將依文件難易，從會員卡使用時數中扣除，請將您需要修改之文章，傳真或郵寄給欣語社。

★ **在校學生英文課業電話輔導** ☎ *(02) 2751-6278*

在系統通話時間，都可依據各級英文（國中、高中、大專院校）內容，為您做文法解析、發音糾正、內容及寫作之討論，加強您聽講能力之課業電話輔導。讓您輕輕鬆鬆應付英文課業，而不再是面對壓力，進而培養學習英文的興趣。

★ **Cassette Telephone Recorder**
（**卡式電話錄放音機；可自行錄製英，日語教學錄音帶**）

適用於桌上型或手提式有線電話，在您跟外籍老師練習會話時，即可利用一般錄音帶做線上雙面錄音；除事後可重複聽帶以加強聽力外，亦可檢討自己發音、文法正確與否？對話內容是否適切？換言之，您可在家裡錄製自己所需之英、日語教學錄音帶，此機除使用於電話外，亦可用作一般之錄音機，如有需要請來電洽詢。

★ **英語會談諮詢，每次 200 元**

每週五下午 7:30 至 9:00，本社現場備有外語助理，可協助會員英語任何方面之請益（因場地有限，只接受空中外語交談園地之會員參與）。您可視需要隨時駕臨，每次酌收費用 NT$200 元。

欣語社
克拉瑪語音廣場
台北市忠孝東路四段 155 號 11 樓之 3
TEL:(02) 2751-6278
FAX:(02) 2751-0017
AM10:00 ～ PM10:00

Editorial Staff

- 修編 / 謝靜芳

- 校訂 / 劉　毅・吳濱伶・蔡琇瑩

- 校閱 / Bruce S. Stewart・Kenyon T. Cotton
  Thomas Deneau

- 美編 / 張鳳儀・吳正順

- 封面設計 / 張鳳儀

- 打字 / 黃淑貞・吳秋香

||||||||||||||| ● 學習出版公司門市部 ● |||||||||||||||

台北地區：台北市許昌街 10 號 2 樓 TEL：(02)2331-4060・2331-9209
台中地區：台中市綠川東街 32 號 8 樓 23 室
　　　　　TEL：(04)223-2838

||||||||||||||||||||||||||||||||||||||||||||||||||||||

電話英語

修　　編／謝靜芳
發　行　所／學習出版有限公司　　　　☎ (02) 2704-5525
郵 撥 帳 號／0512727-2 學習出版社帳戶
登　記　證／局版台業 2179 號
印　刷　所／裕強彩色印刷有限公司
台 北 門 市／台北市許昌街 10 號 2 F　　☎ (02) 2331-4060・2331-9209
台 中 門 市／台中市綠川東街 32 號 8 F 23 室　　☎ (04) 223-2838
台灣總經銷／學英文化事業公司　　　☎ (02) 2218-7307
美國總經銷／ Evergreen Book Store　☎ (818) 2813622

售價：新台幣一百五十元正
1998 年 10 月 1 日二版二刷

ISBN 957-519-182-X